Hidden IMAGES

VEHICLES

THE ULTIMATE COLORING EXPERIENCE

ROGER BURROWS

To my youngest son, Nick.

Printed in China

9   8   7   6   5   4   3   2   1
Digit on the right indicates the number of this printing

Library of Congress Catalog Control Number: 2009943428

ISBN 978-0-7624-3950-8

Cover design by Ryan Hayes
Edited by Jordana Tusman
Typography: Verlag

Published by Running Press Kids
an imprint of Running Press Book Publishers
2300 Chestnut Street
Philadelphia, PA 19103-4371

Visit us on the web!
www.runningpress.com

Hidden IMAGES
VEHICLES
THE ULTIMATE COLORING EXPERIENCE

ROGER BURROWS

RP | KIDS
PHILADELPHIA • LONDON

INTRODUCTION

The designs in this book were created to stimulate the visual imagination. When you look at each design, relax your vision and search for large and small images, complete scenes, or abstract patterns. Any shape that you find can be found again and again in the same direction, but also rotated and reflected. Designs are repeated so you can explore images in different ways, but the images are only intended as starting points. Use the visual examples given to discover cars, trucks, trains, and all different kinds of vehicles, but use your imagination to find images and patterns on your own.

Use felt pens, colored pencils, markers, pastels, or even paints to color within lines or across them. You can use shading, textures, or solid colors. You can even choose to enlarge the designs onto fabric, wood, or canvas. You may want to frame some of the designs, or use them for greeting cards, decorations, and presents. The possibilities are limitless. Please visit my website at www.rogerburrowsimages.com.

Hope you enjoy this book!

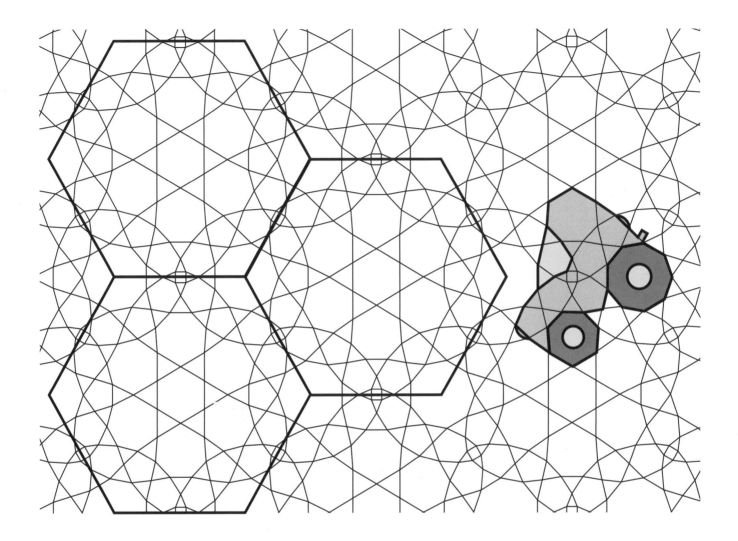

All of the designs in this book are based on close-packing circles. Six close-packed circles are positioned within a right-angle triangle. The triangle is reflected and rotated to create a hexagon, and the hexagon tessellates to cover the plane.

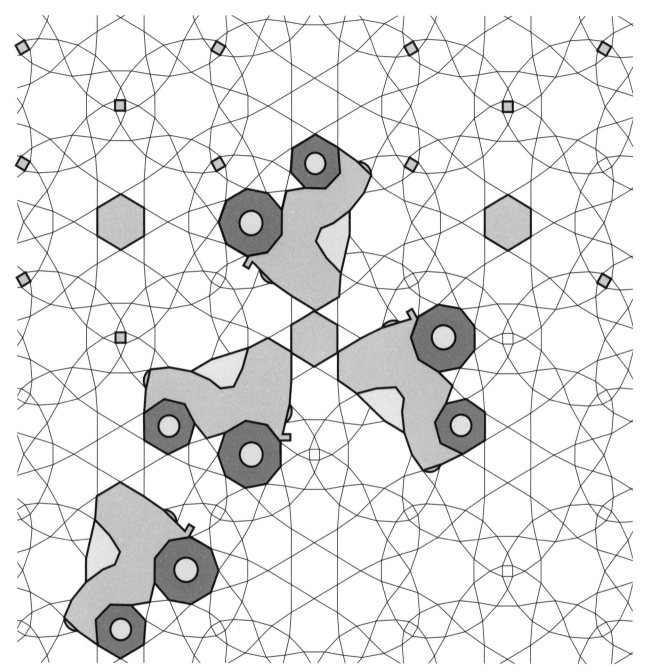

DESIGN # 1

In each design, you will find simple shapes that repeat, like the hexagons and squares above. You will find that an image, like the car, will repeat and rotate around these simple shapes. Find the shapes in the design on the right, then look for the cars.

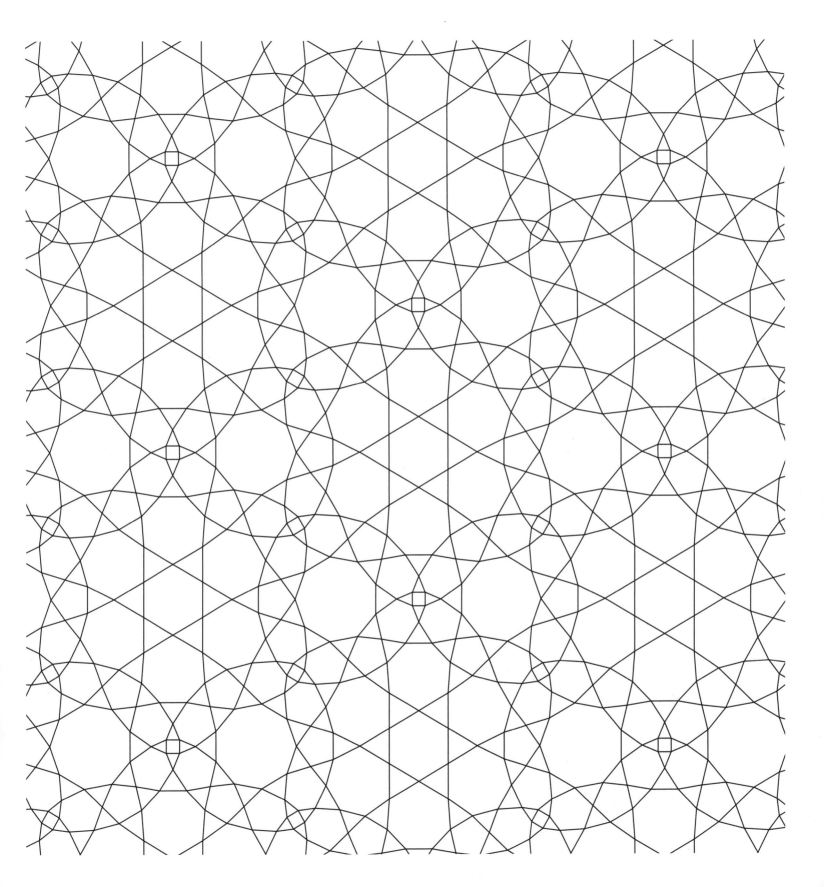

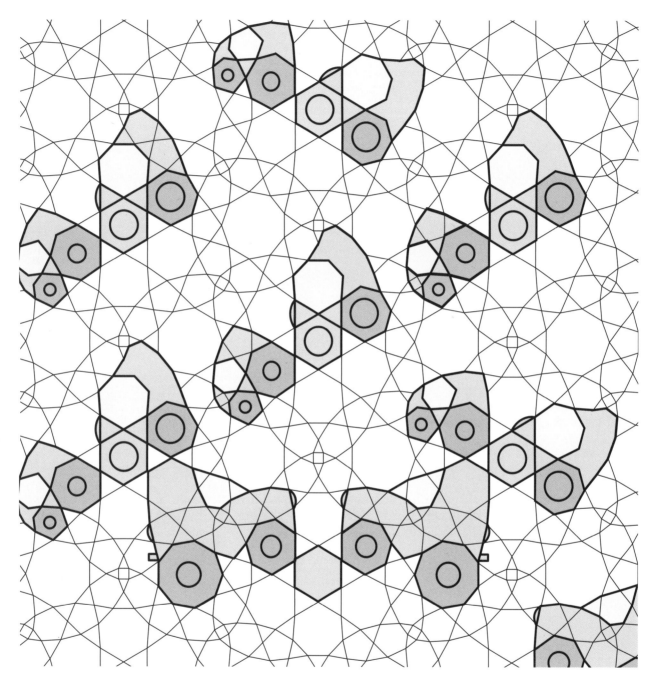

DESIGN # 1

Look for the hexagons in the design on the right. See if you can find the cars that repeat next to them.

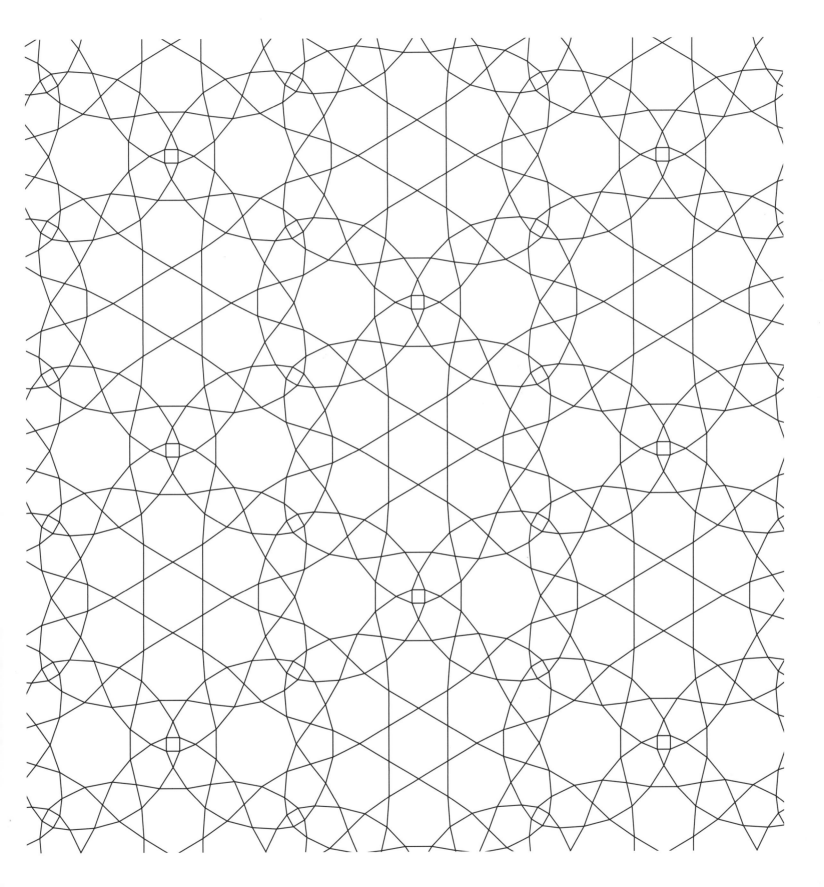

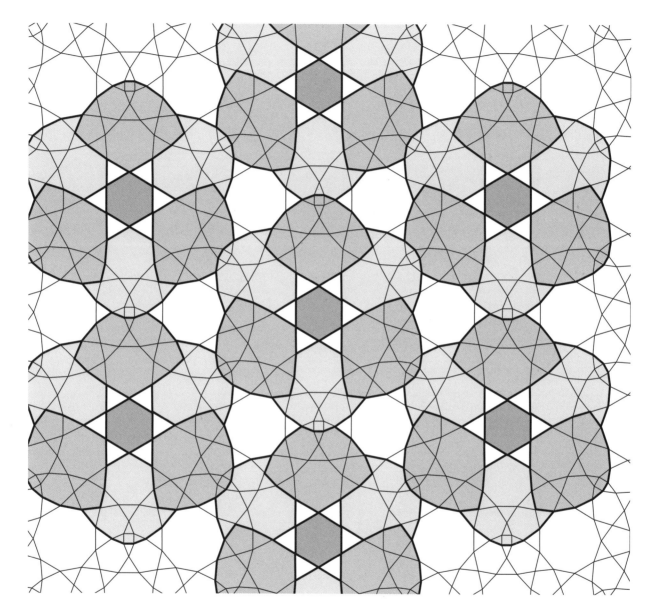

DESIGN # 1

Create patterns from shapes so you can easily find images. What images can you find?

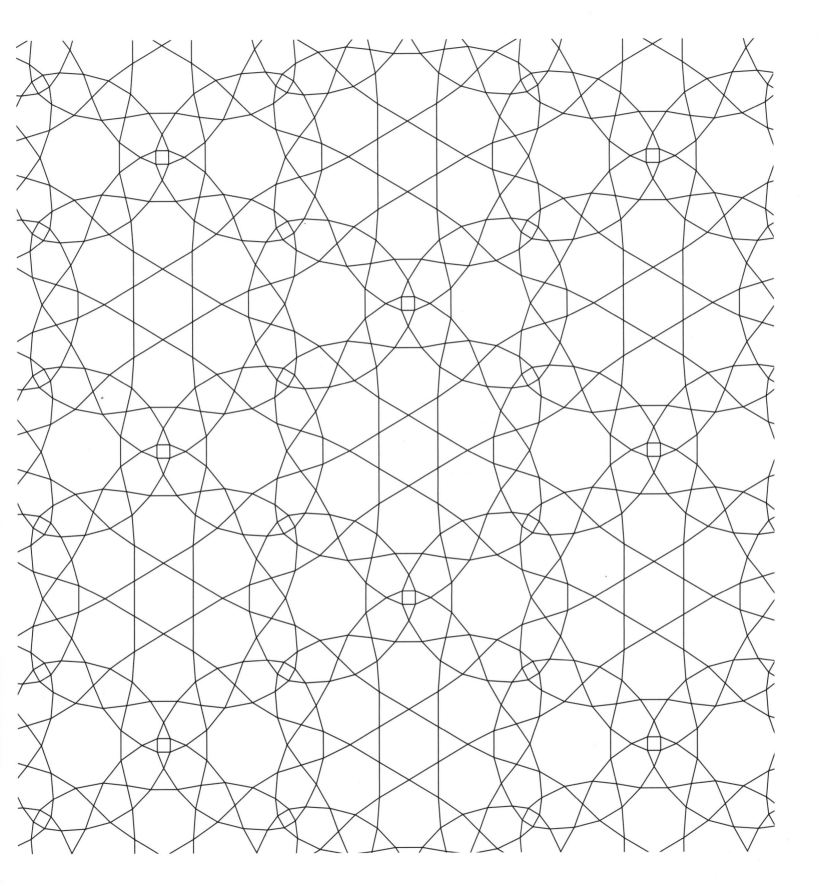

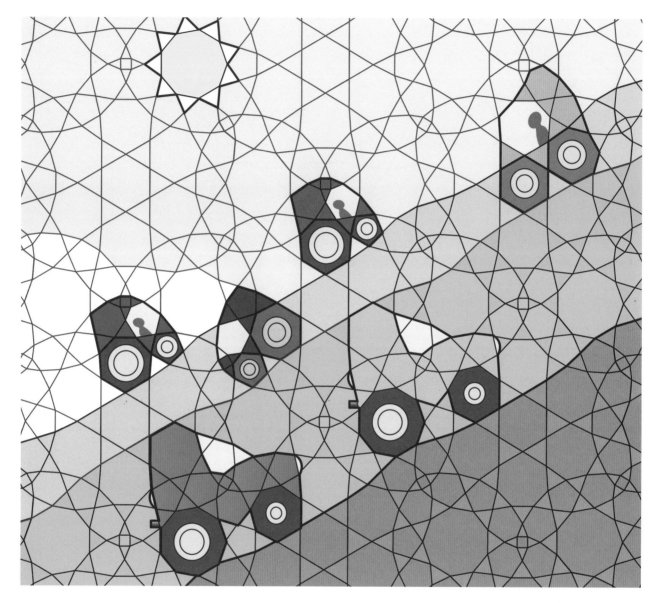

DESIGN # 1

You can create complete scenes with the images you find. Can you add some hills and a sun in the design on the right?

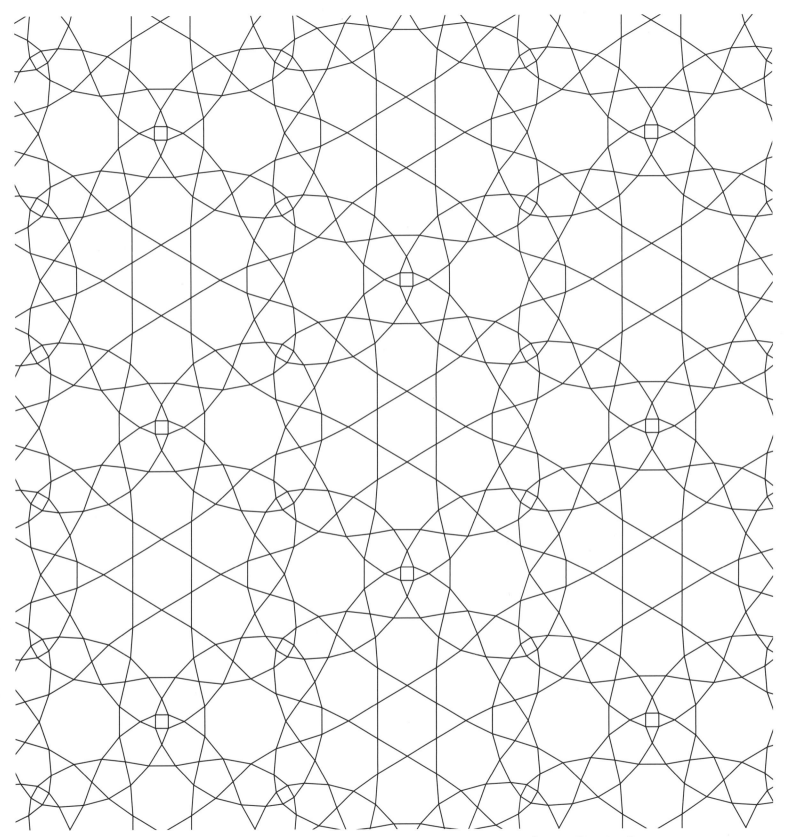

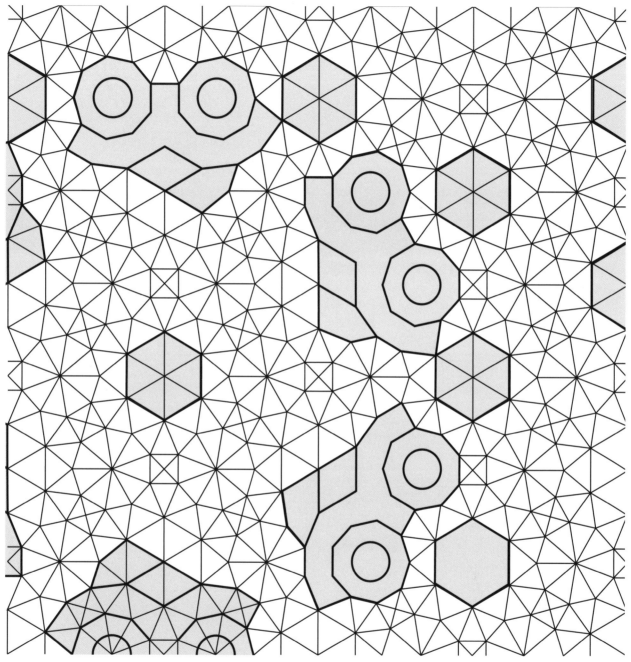

DESIGN # 2

When you find the repeating hexagons, you can find the cars next to them.

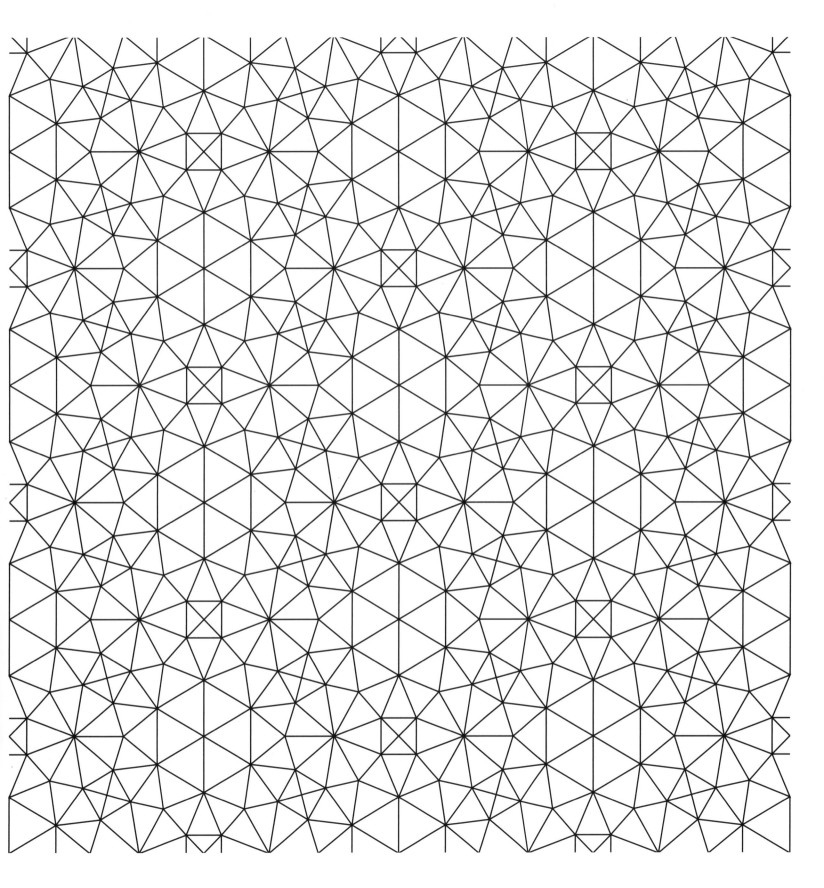

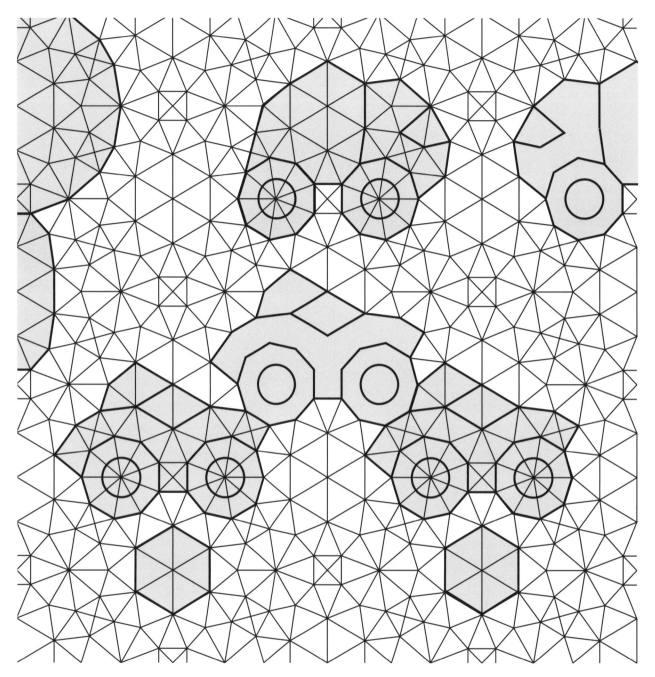

DESIGN # 2

Can you find trucks?

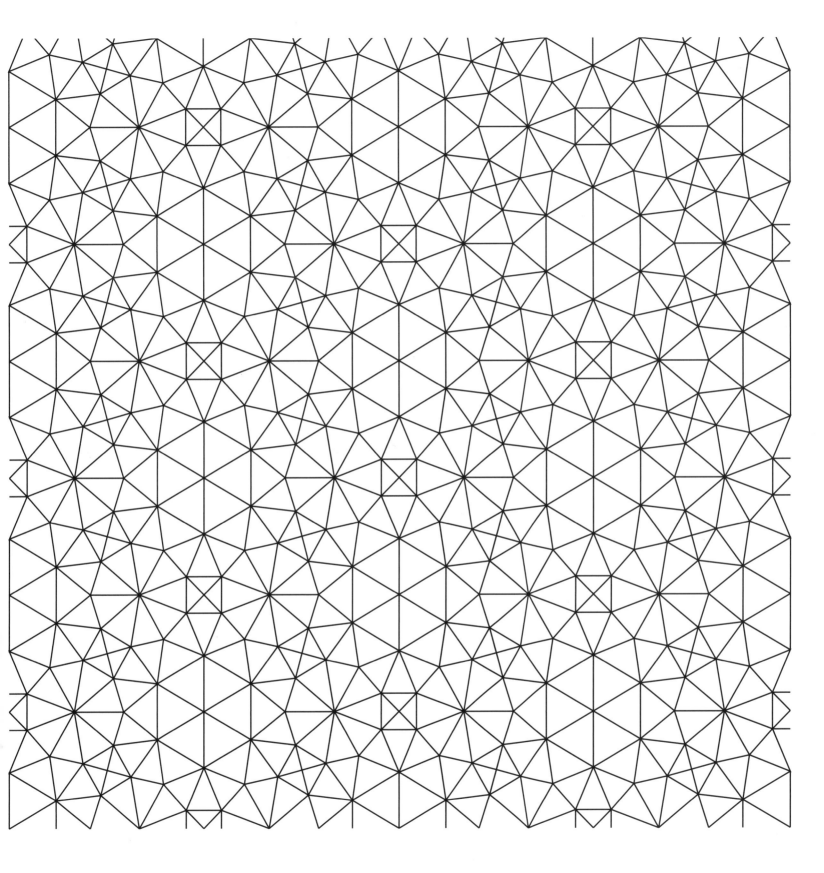

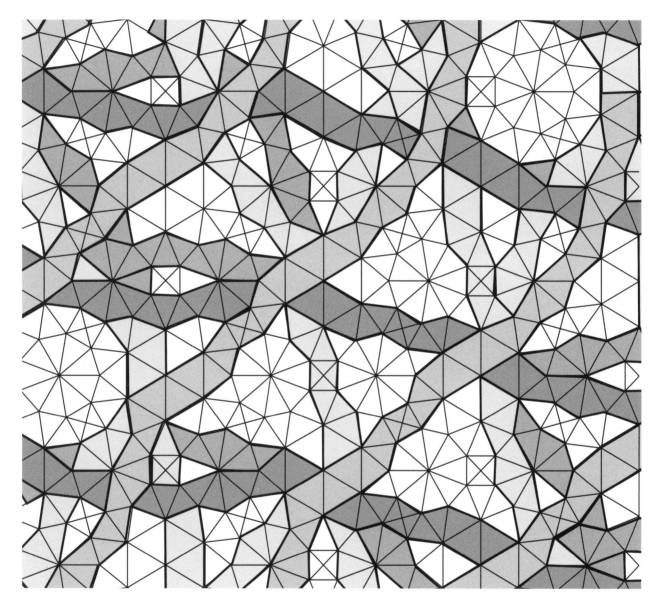

DESIGN # 2

What other images do you see in the patterns? Can you find small and large trees? Can you find a sun?

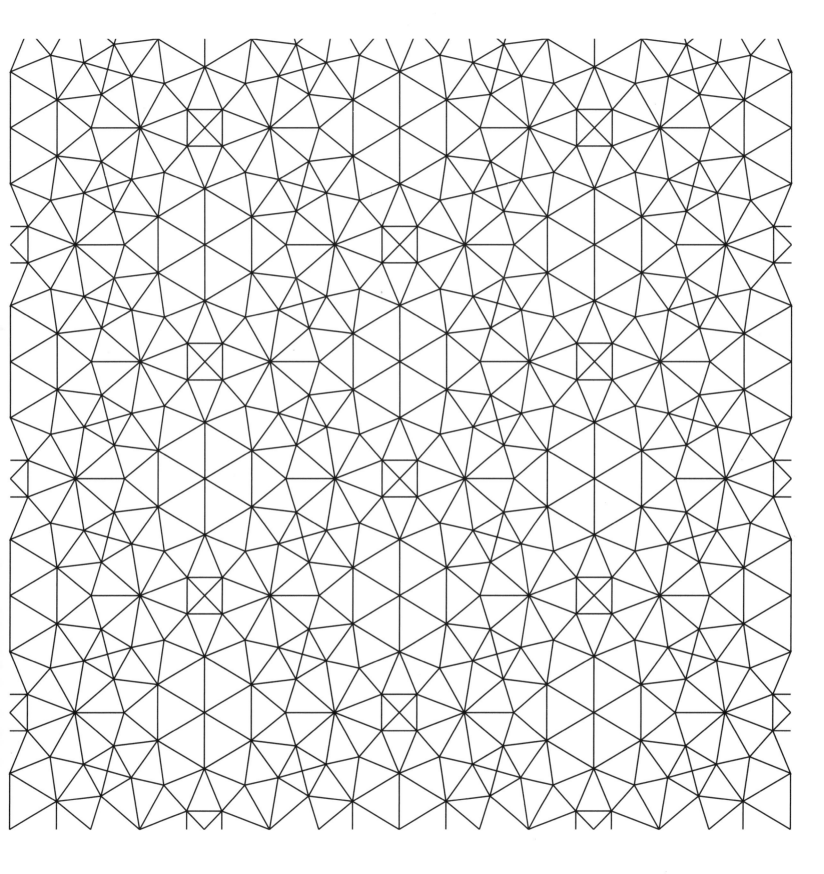

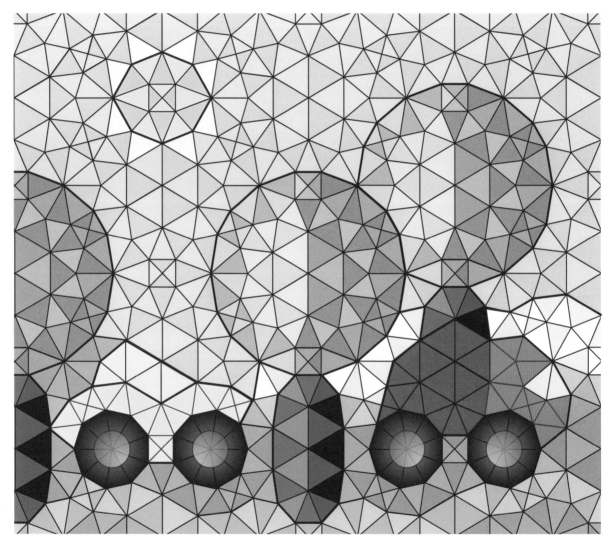

DESIGN # 2

Combine the images you find to make a finished scene.

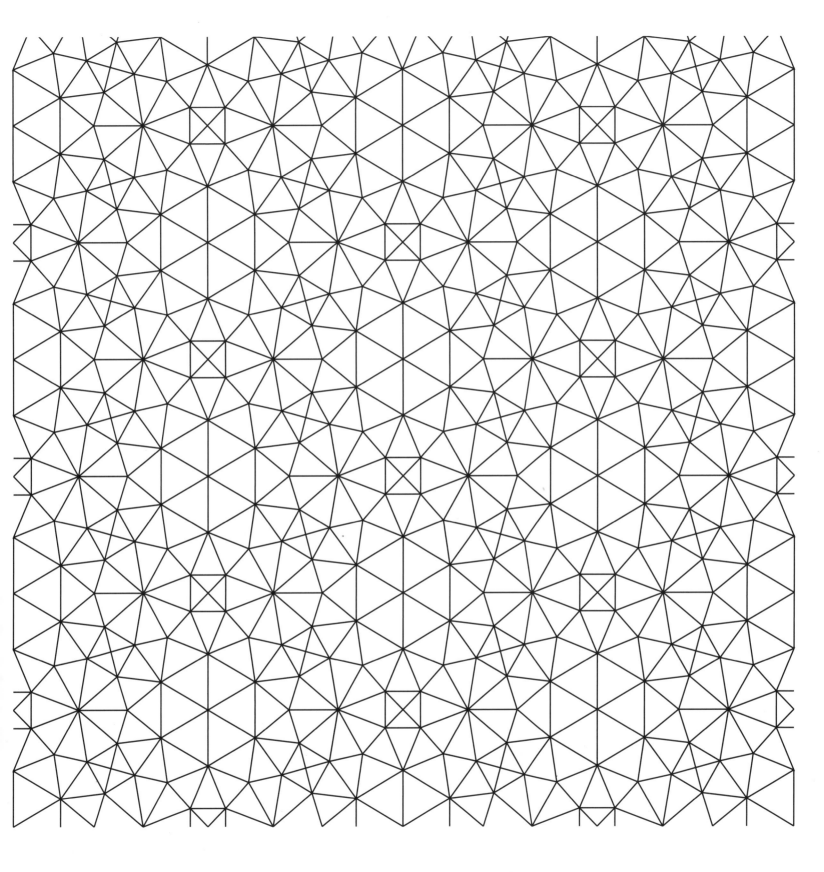

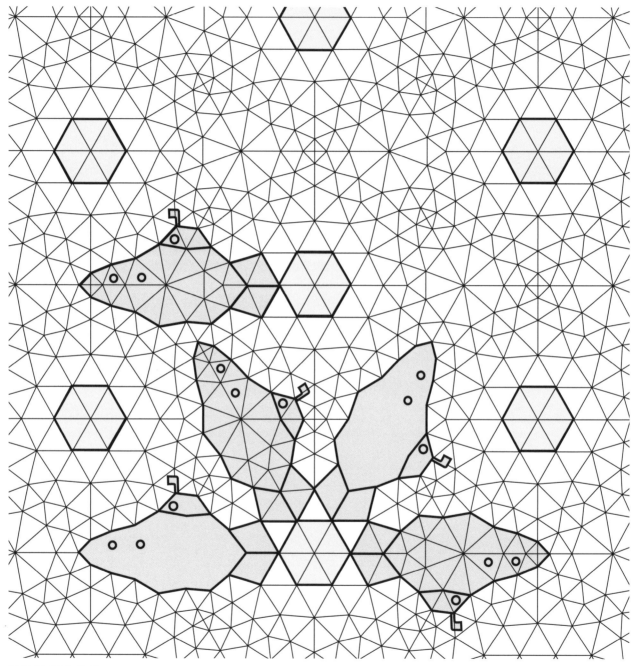

DESIGN # 3

Locate the hexagons to help you find the submarines.

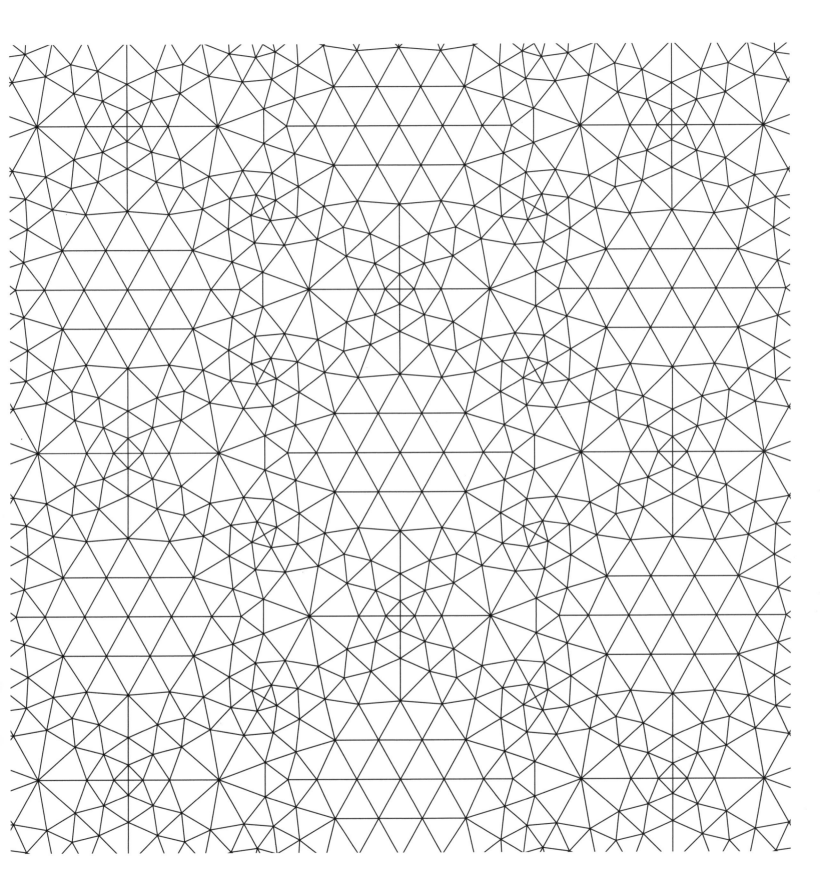

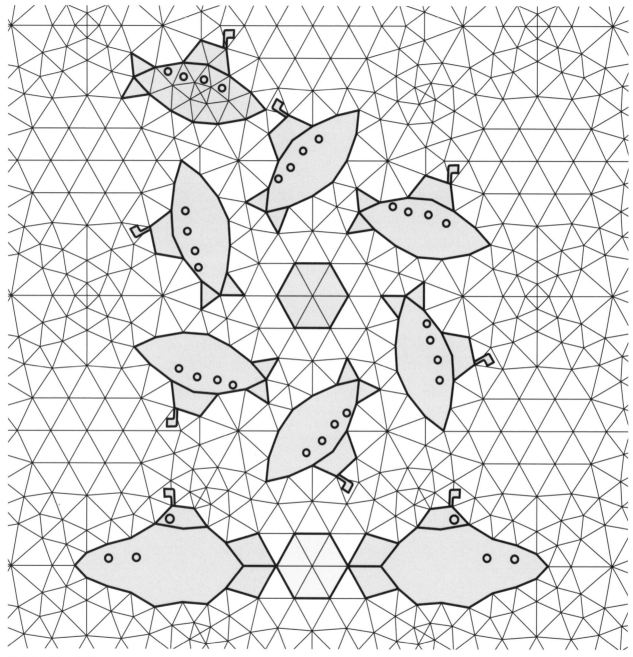

DESIGN # 3

Notice how the submarines rotate and repeat around the hexagons?

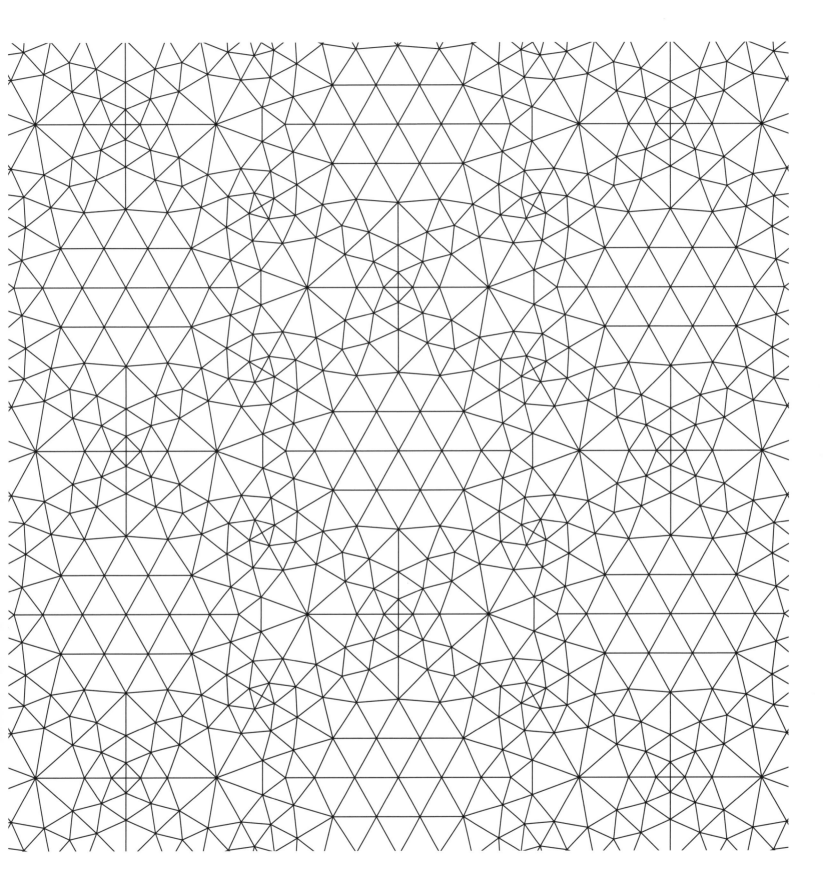

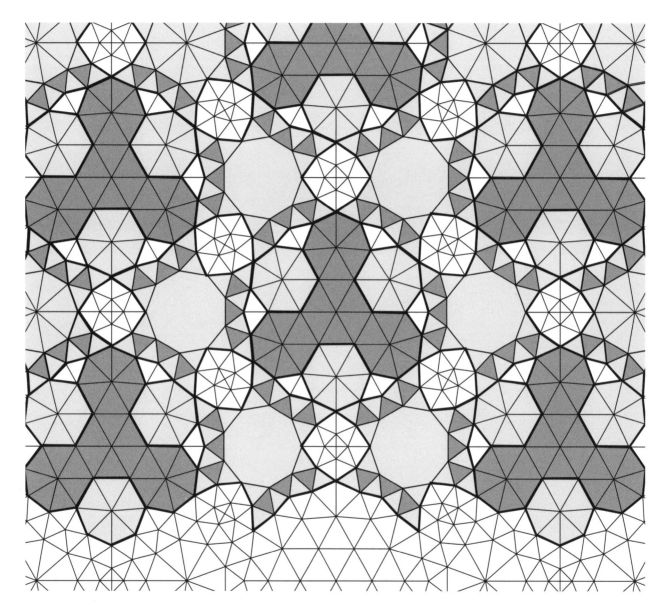

DESIGN # 3

Study the design to find your own shapes and patterns.

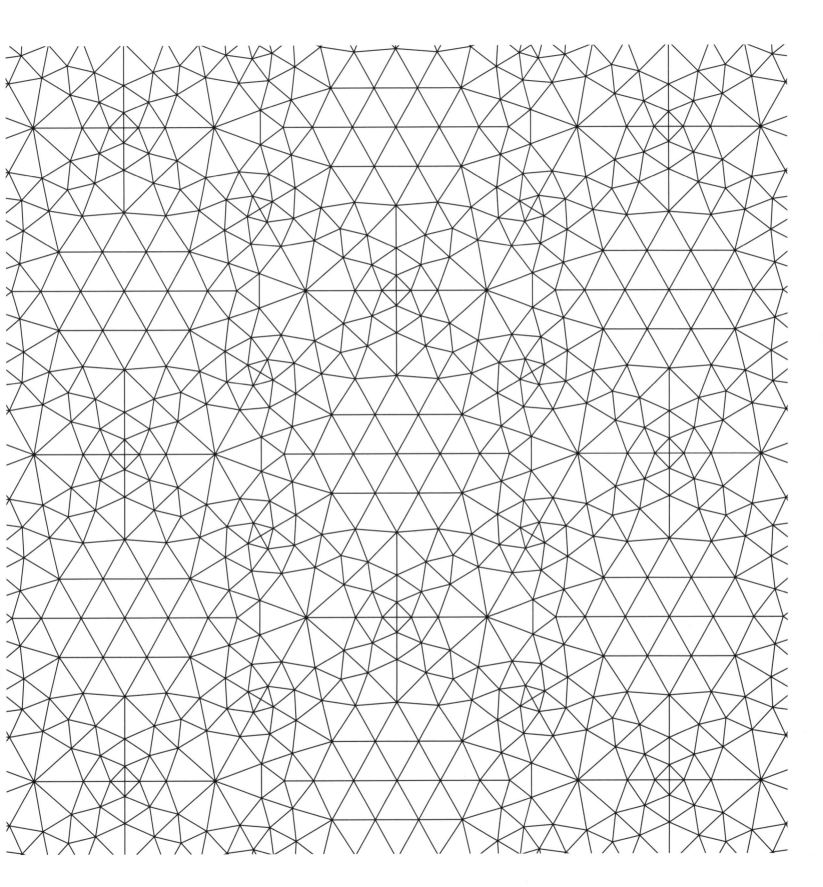

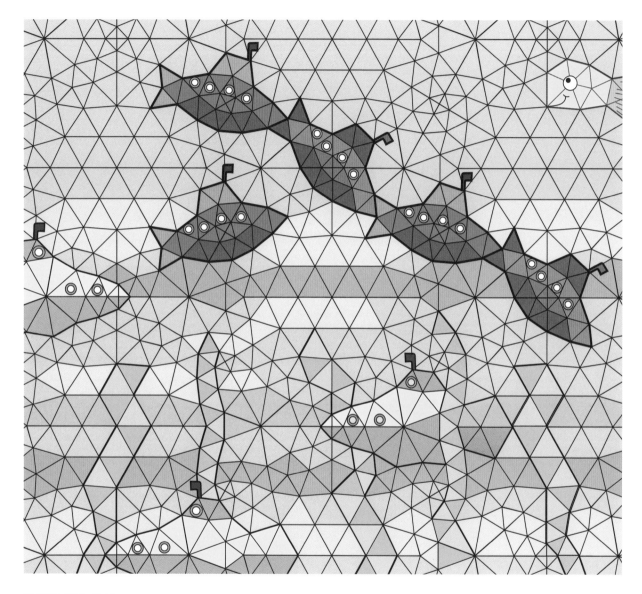

DESIGN # 3

Create a complete scene with all of the images.

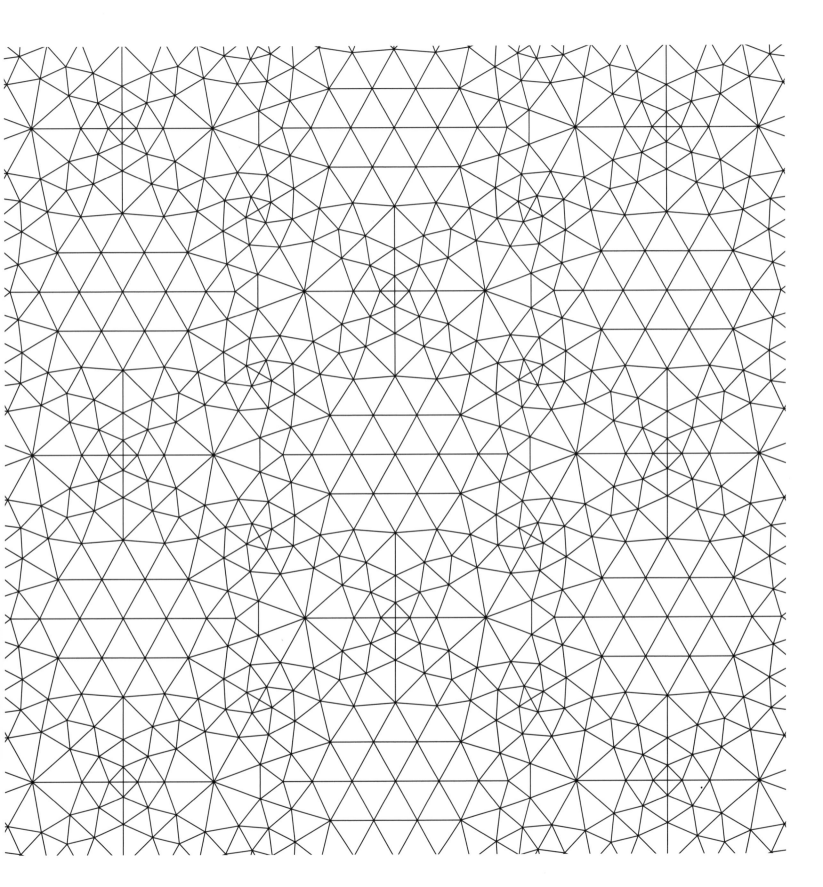

DESIGN # 4

Find the airplanes rotating around the six-sided stars.

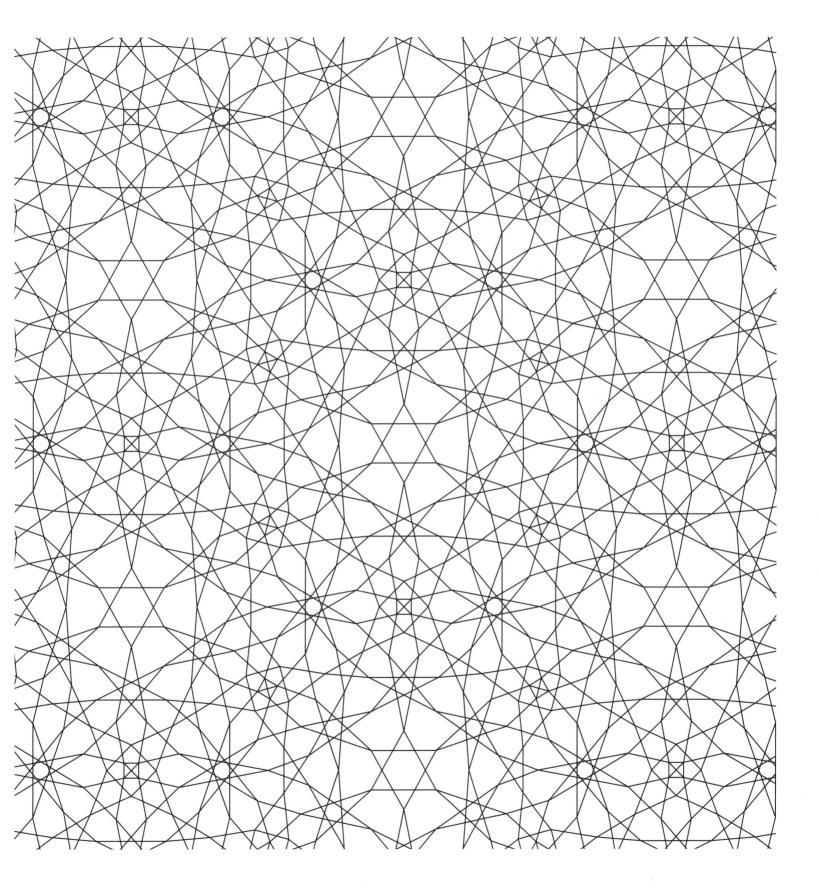

DESIGN # 4

Now that you know how to find airplanes, can you find hot air balloons?

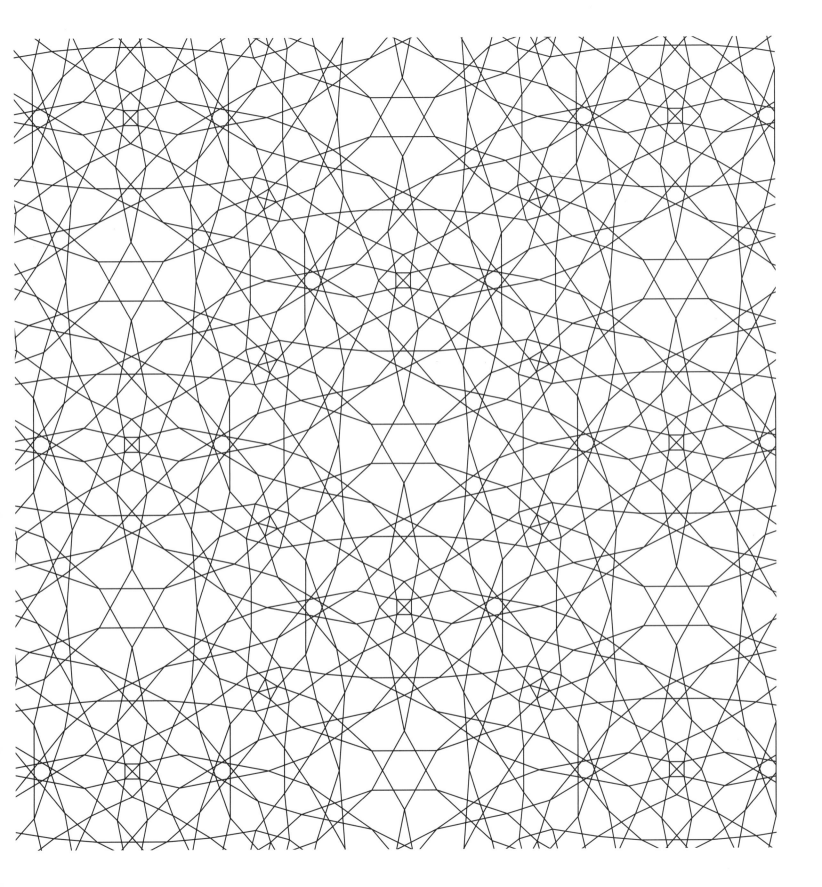

DESIGN # 4

Locate a central point in the design and see how many images you can find.

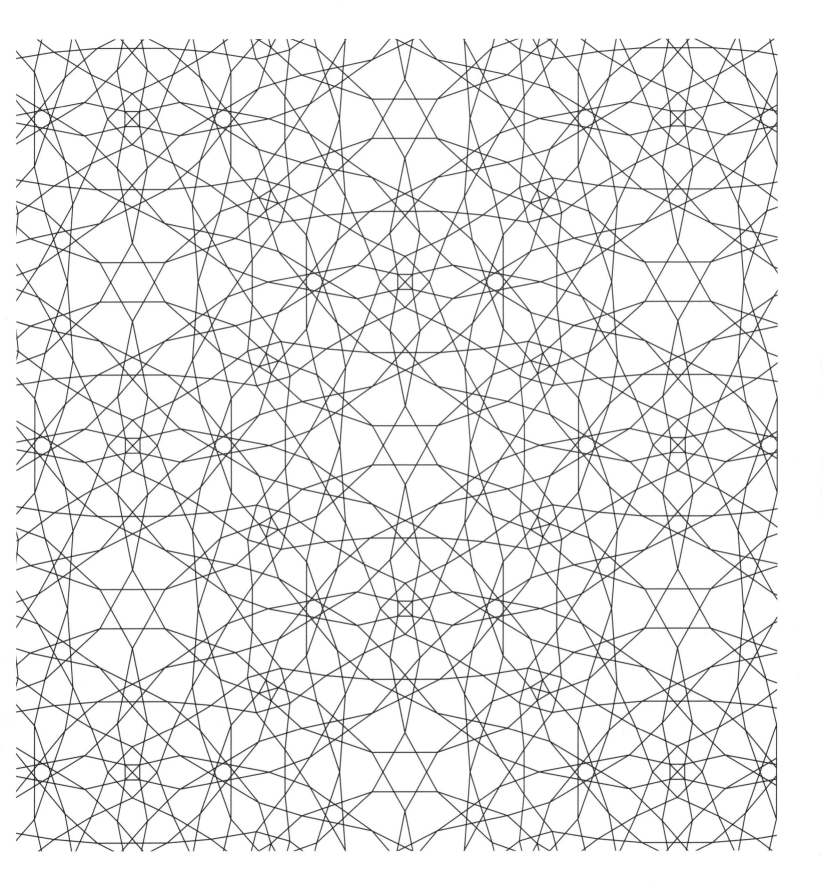

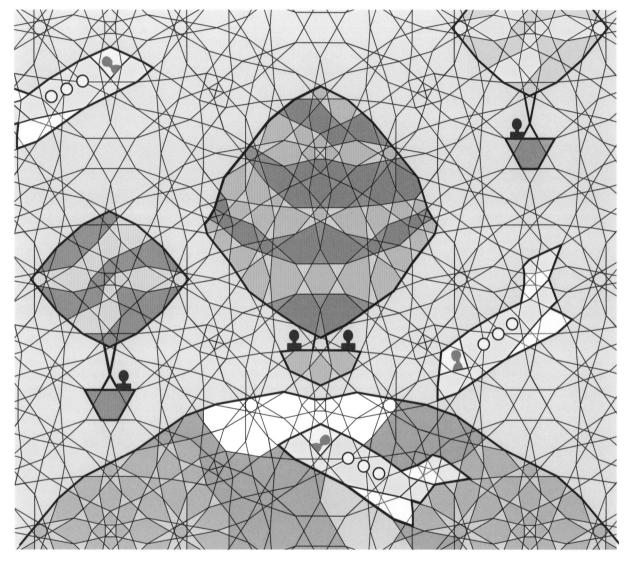

DESIGN # 4

I created this scene with the images that I found. Find planet Earth or other hidden images.

DESIGN # 5

Find trains rotating around the hexagons and squares.

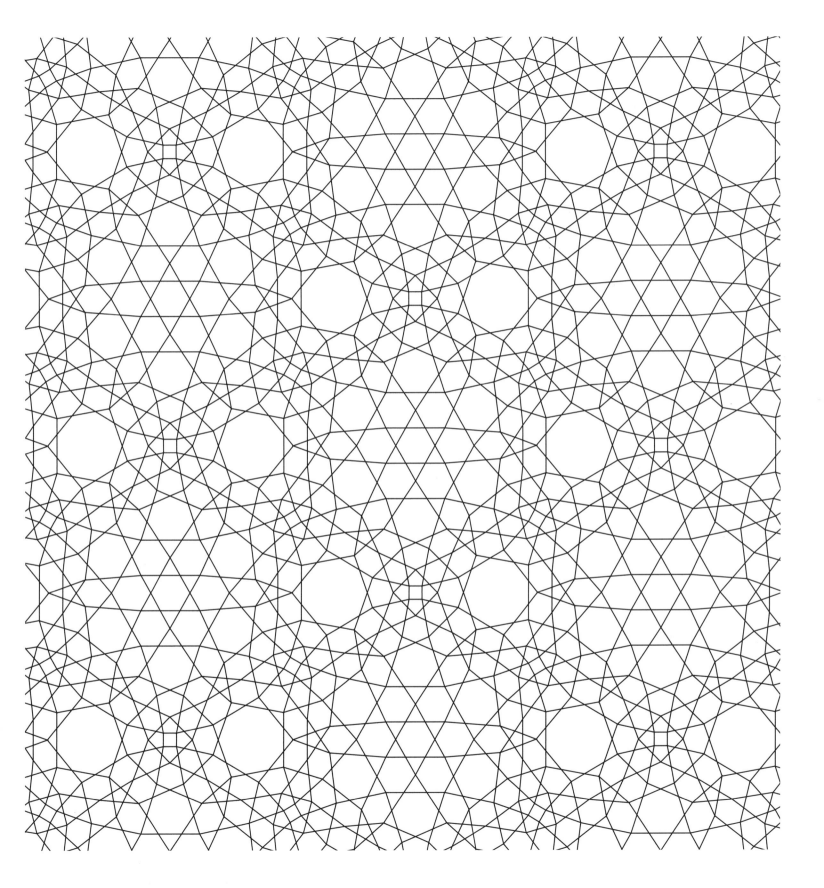

DESIGN # 5

Can you use the squares to help you find the trains in the design on the right?

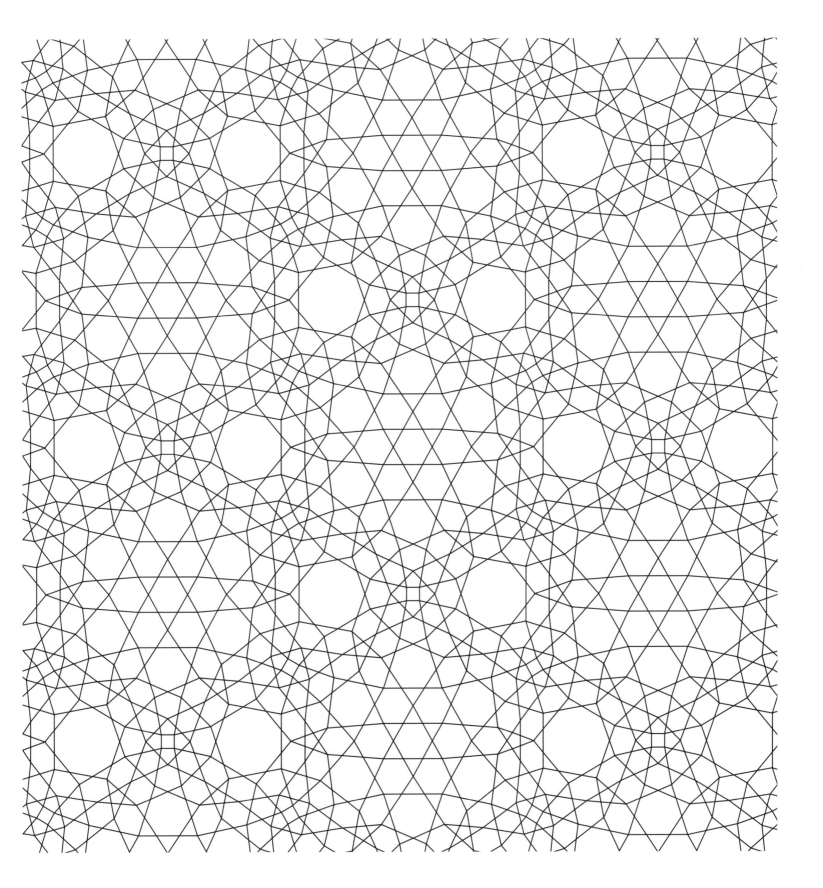

DESIGN # 5

Use shapes and patterns to find images on your own.

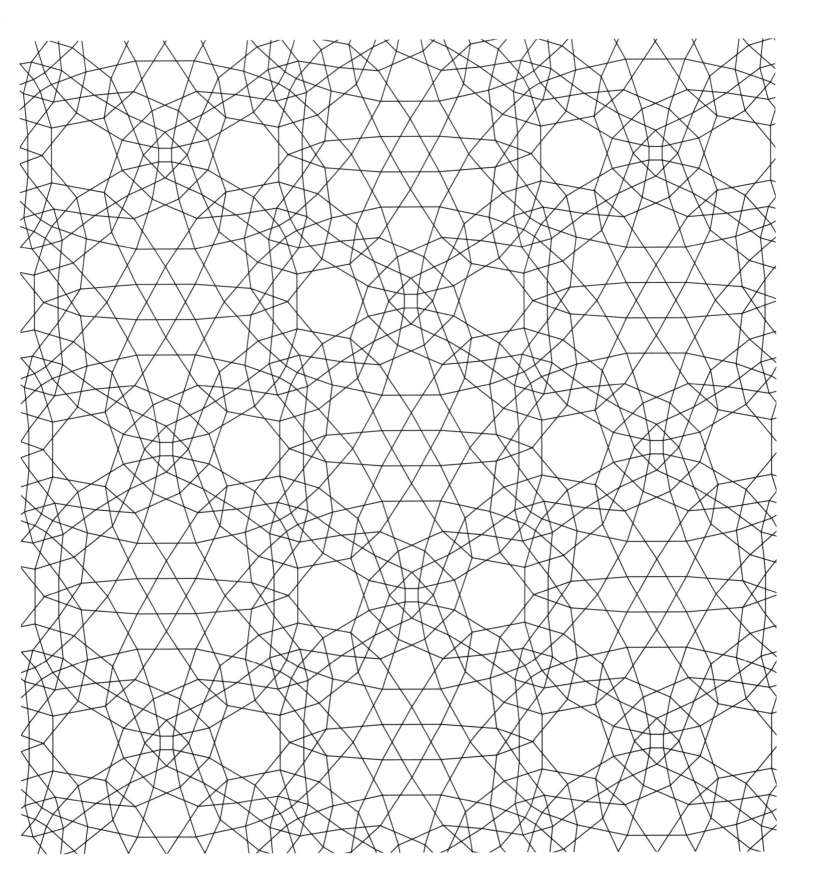

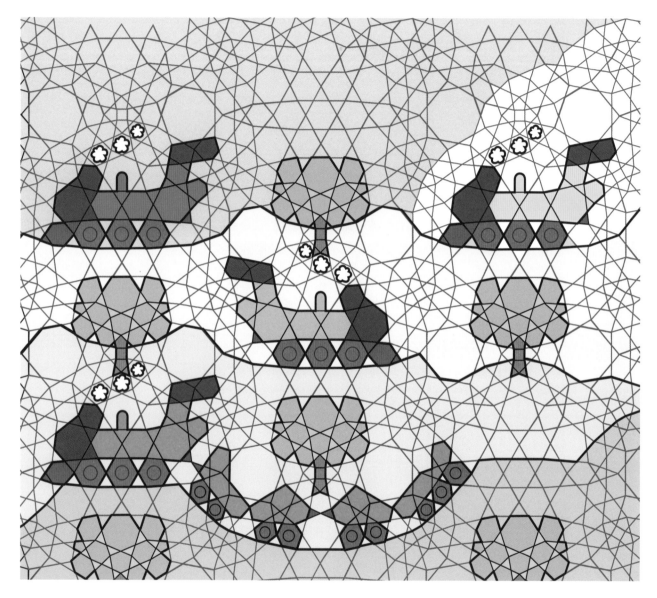

DESIGN # 5

Here is a finished scene combining trains, trees, and hills. Place these images in different positions in the design on the right.

DESIGN # 6

Can you see spaceships and planets in the design?

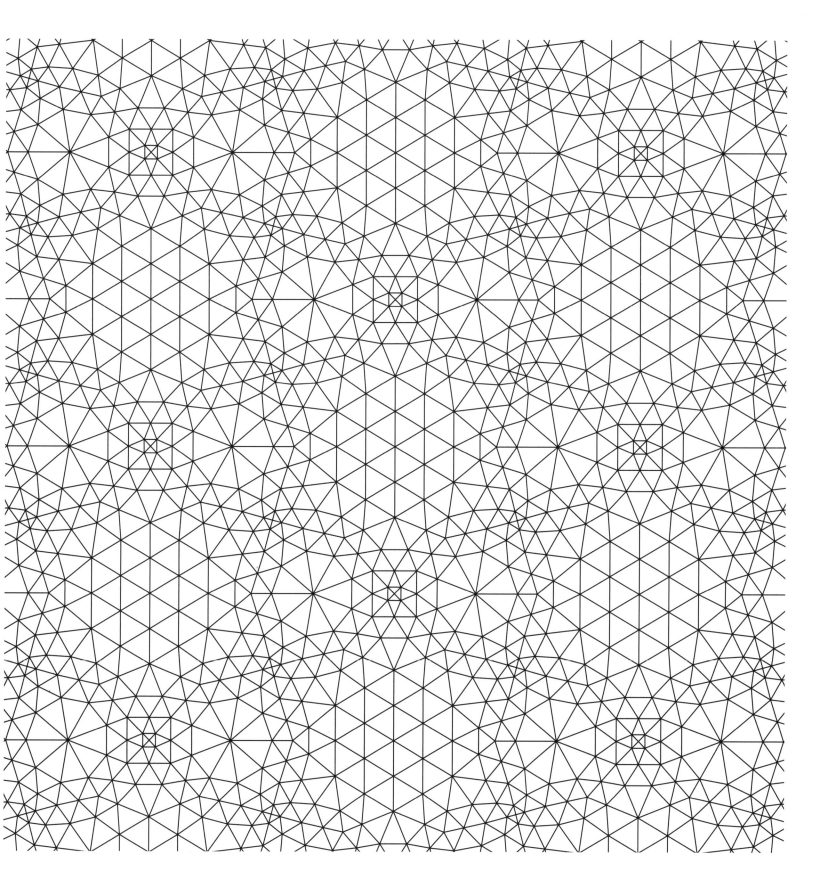

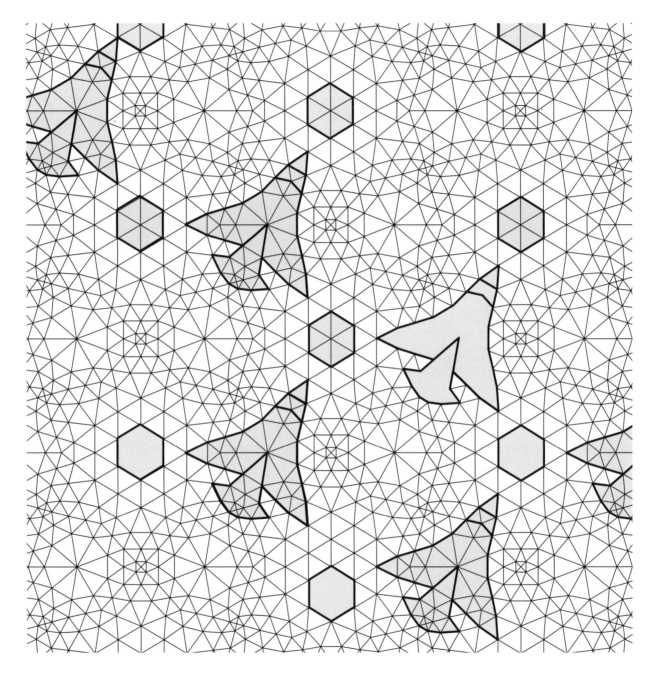

DESIGN # 6

Use shapes like the hexagons to help you find spaceships.

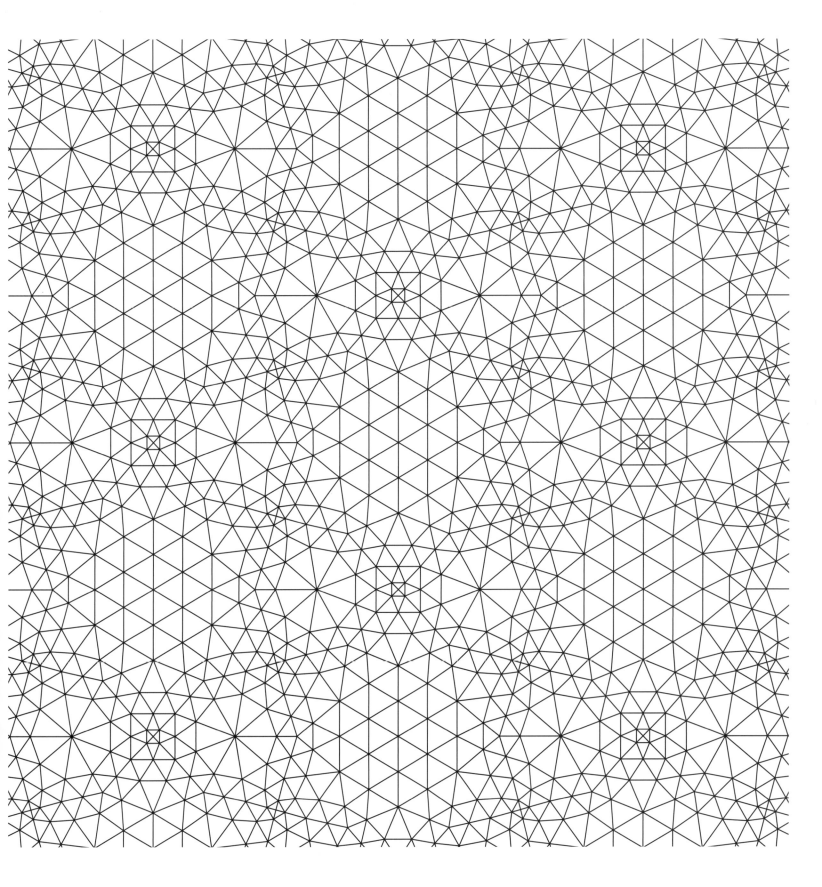

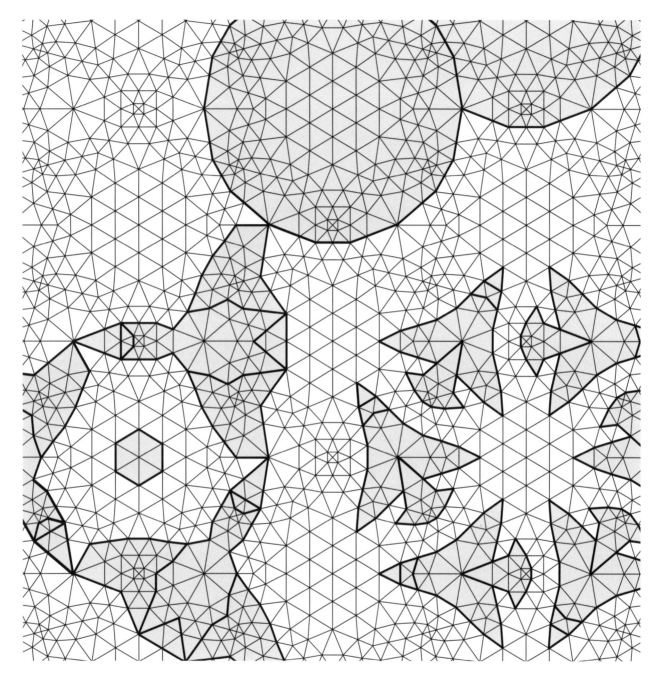

DESIGN # 6

You can also find planets.

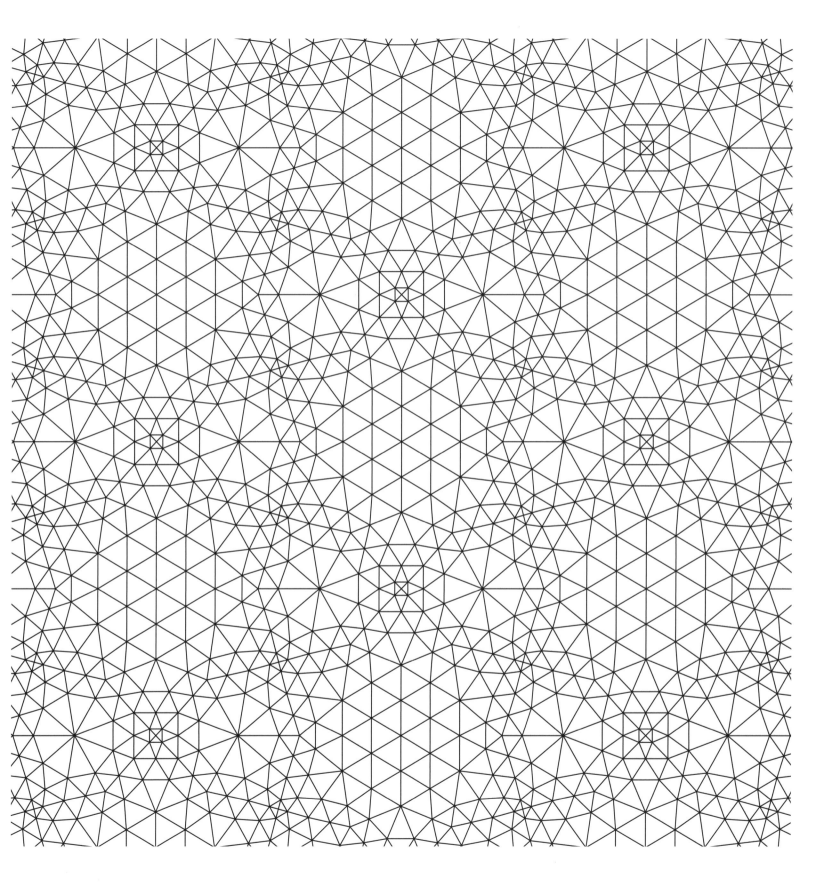

DESIGN # 6

Create spaceships, planets, and stars for the final scene.

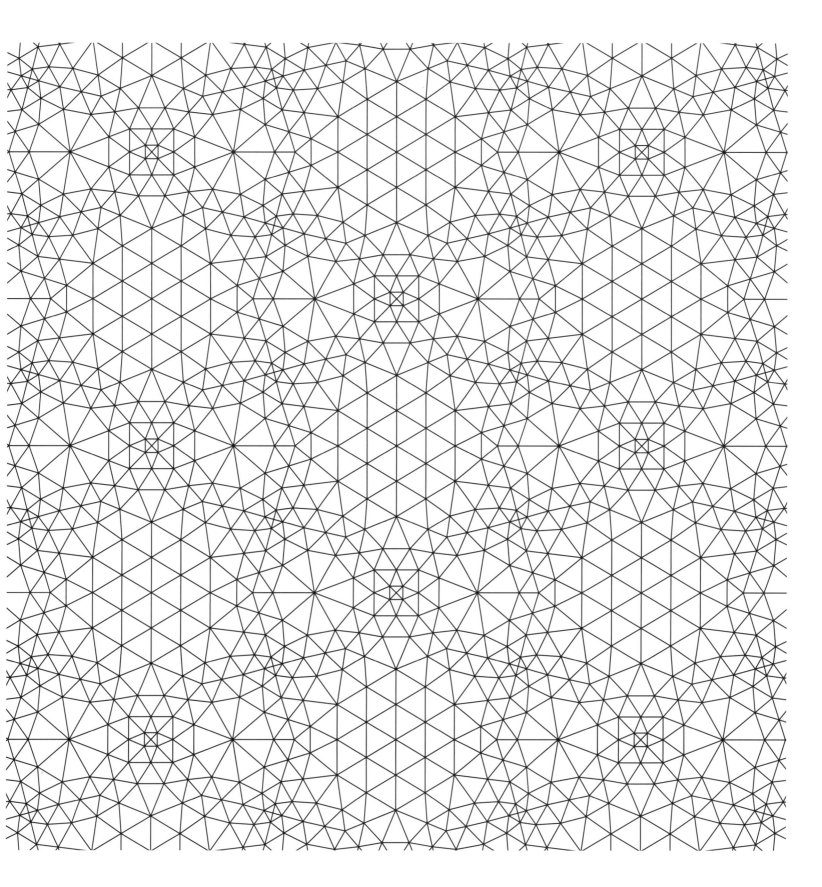

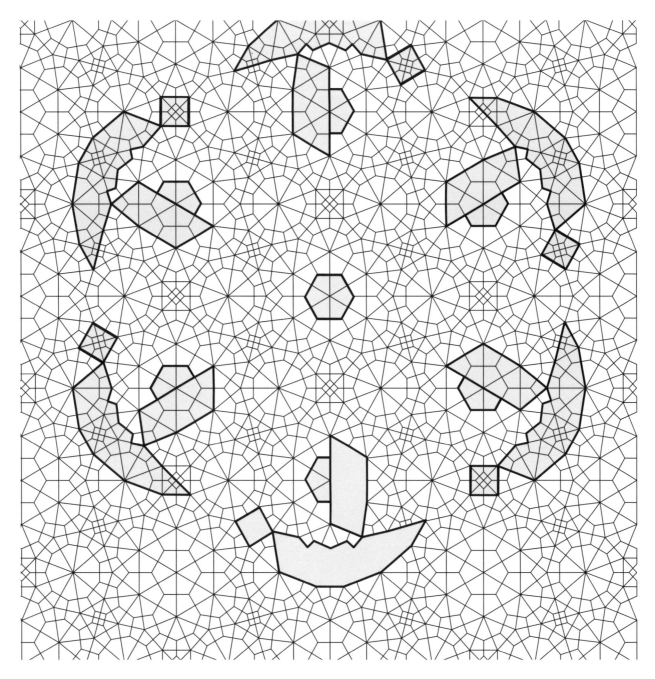

DESIGN # 7

See how the sailboats rotate around the hexagon?

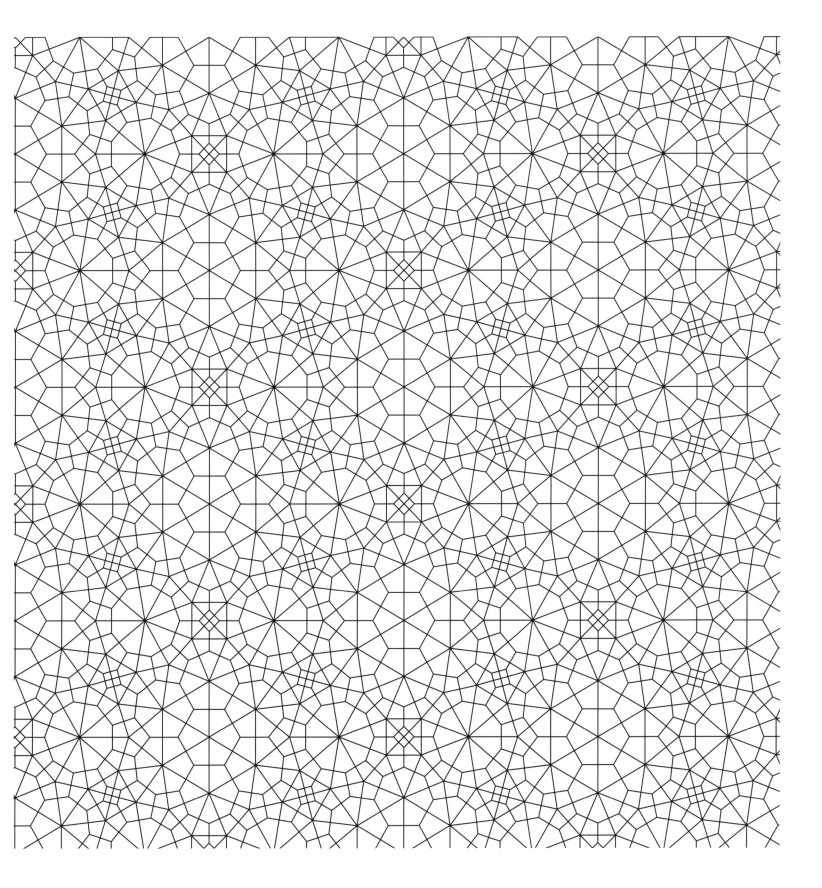

DESIGN # 7

After you find the sailboats, see if you can find hot air balloons and helicopters.

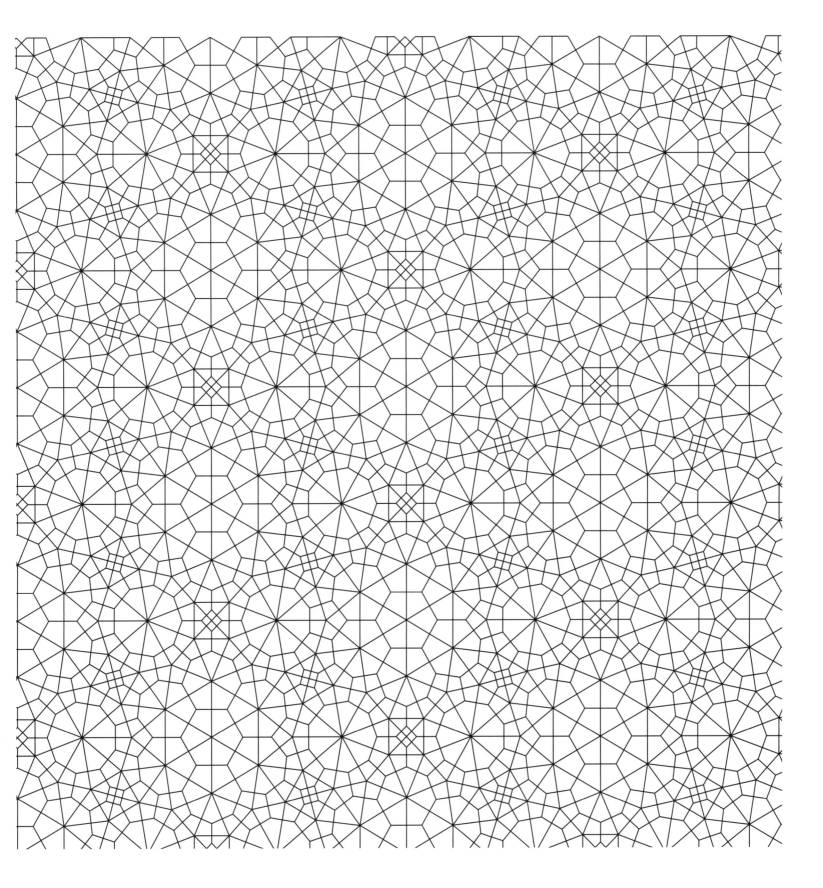

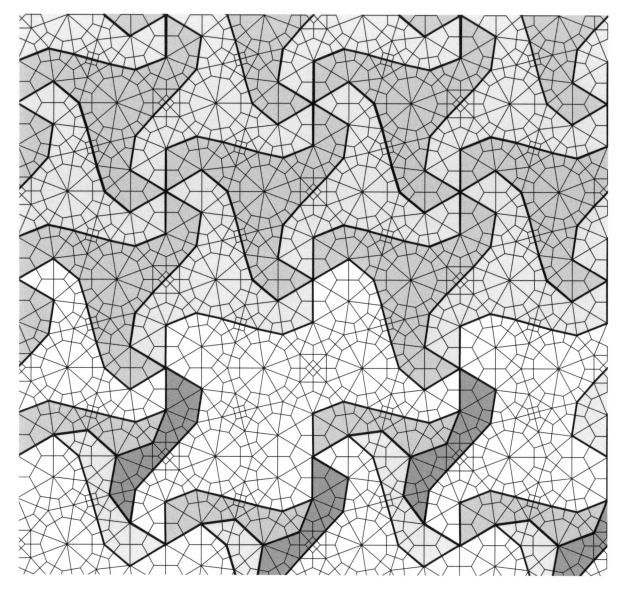

DESIGN # 7

Are there other images that you see in the repeating patterns?

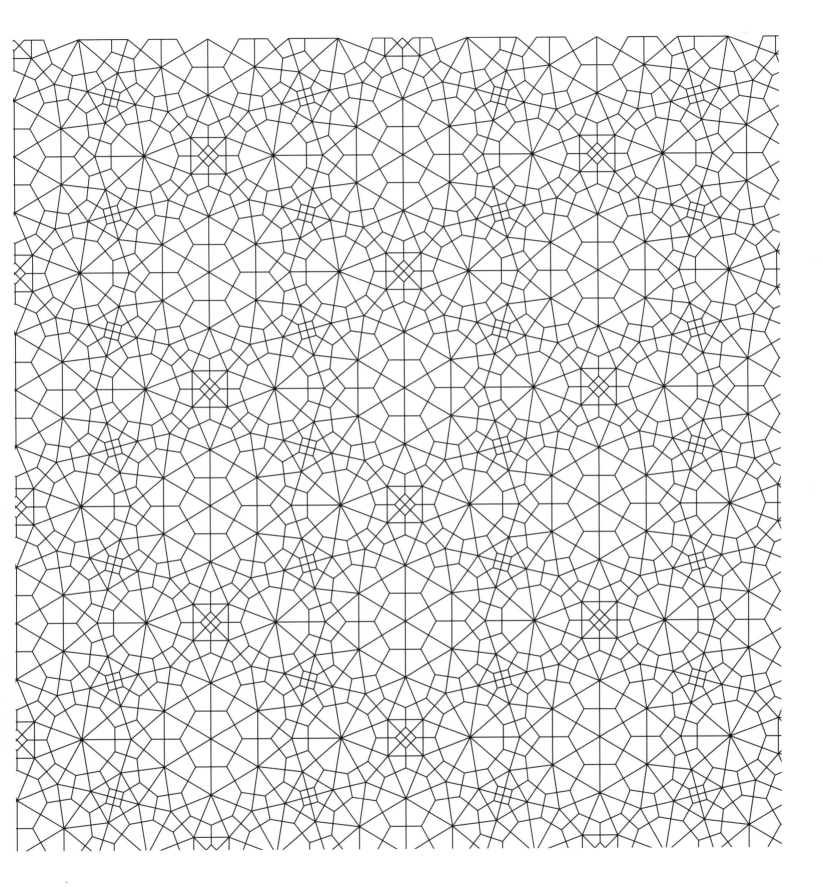

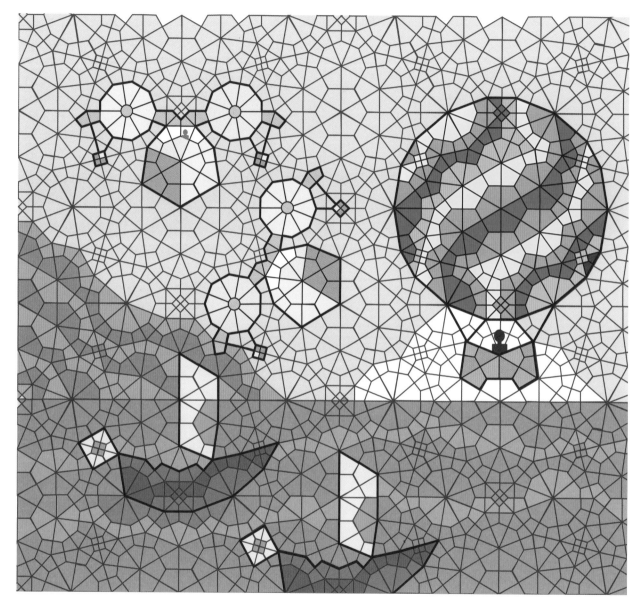

DESIGN # 7

How many sailboats, hot air balloons, and helicopters will you include in the finished scene?

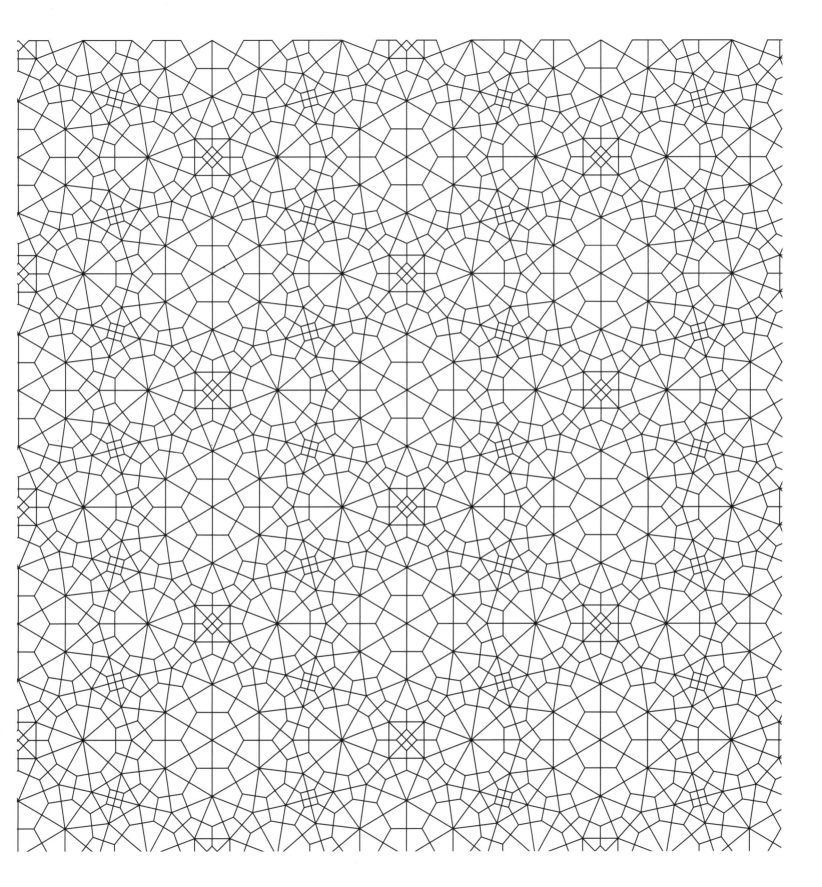

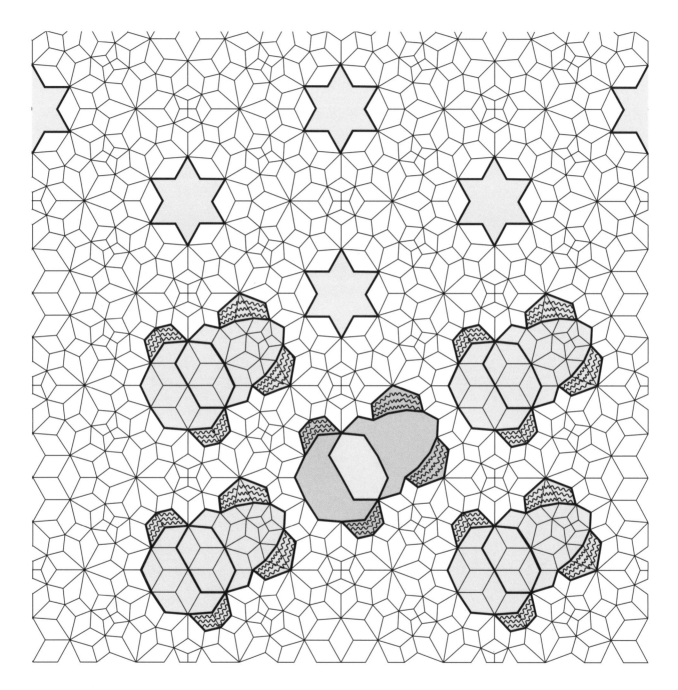

DESIGN # 8

Use the six-sided stars to help you find cars in the design.

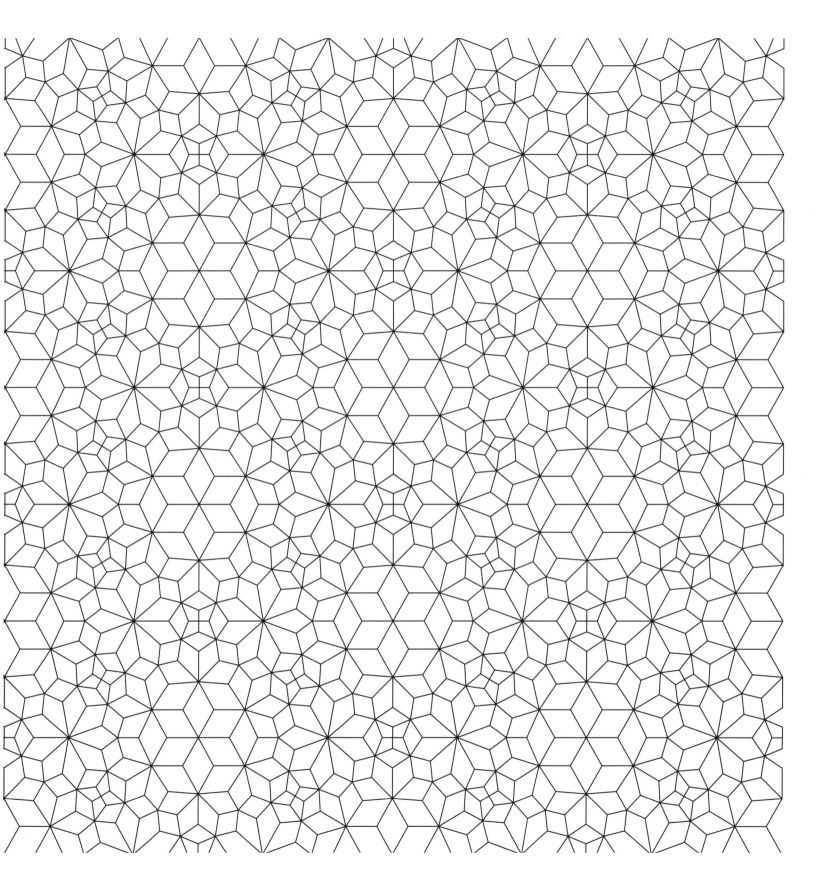

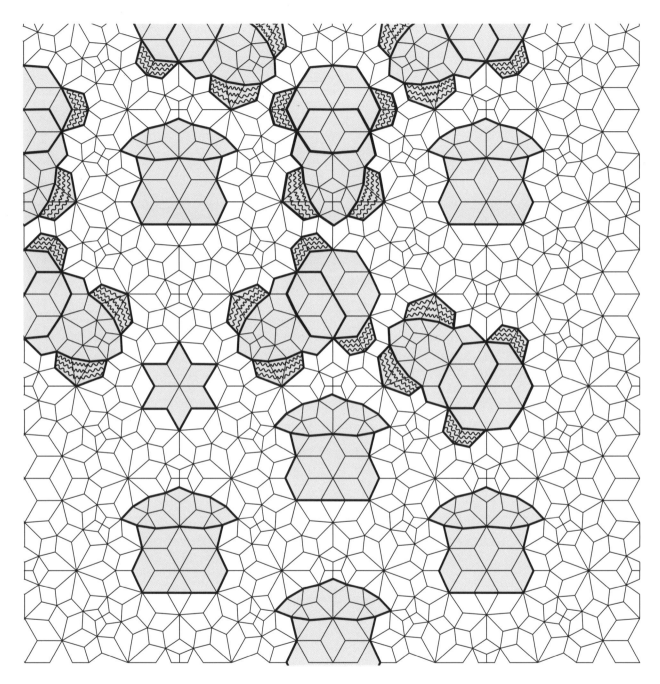

DESIGN # 8

Can you also find houses?

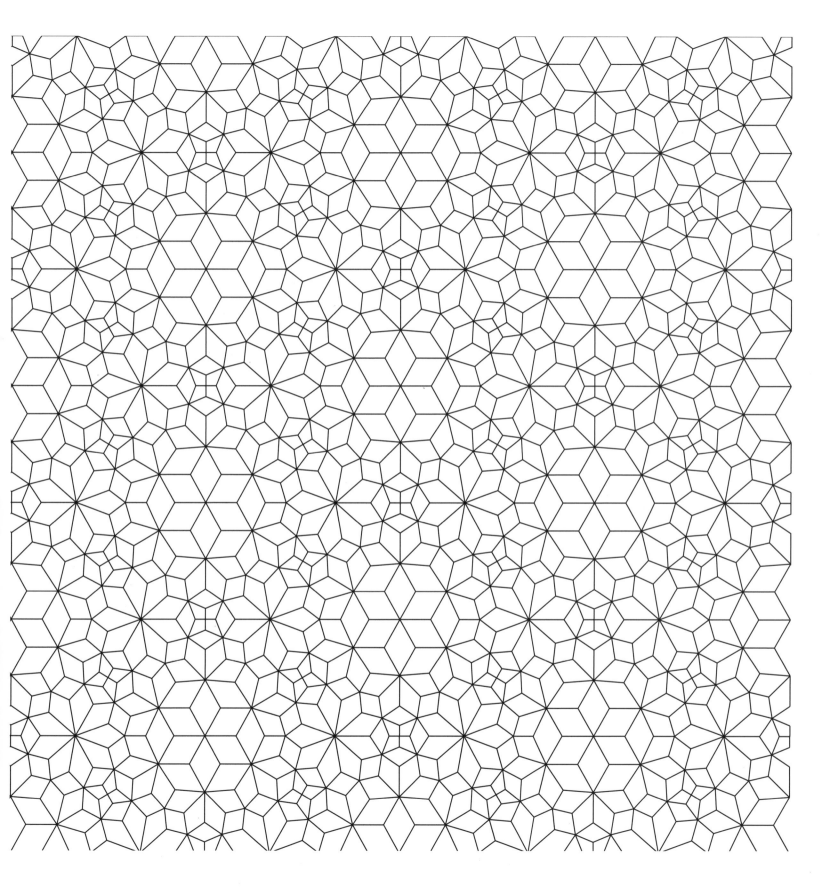

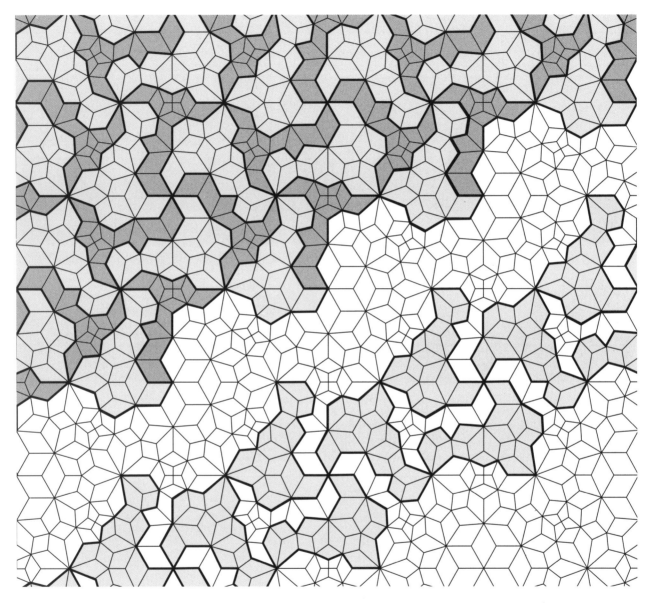

DESIGN # 8

What images can you find in the design by studying patterns?

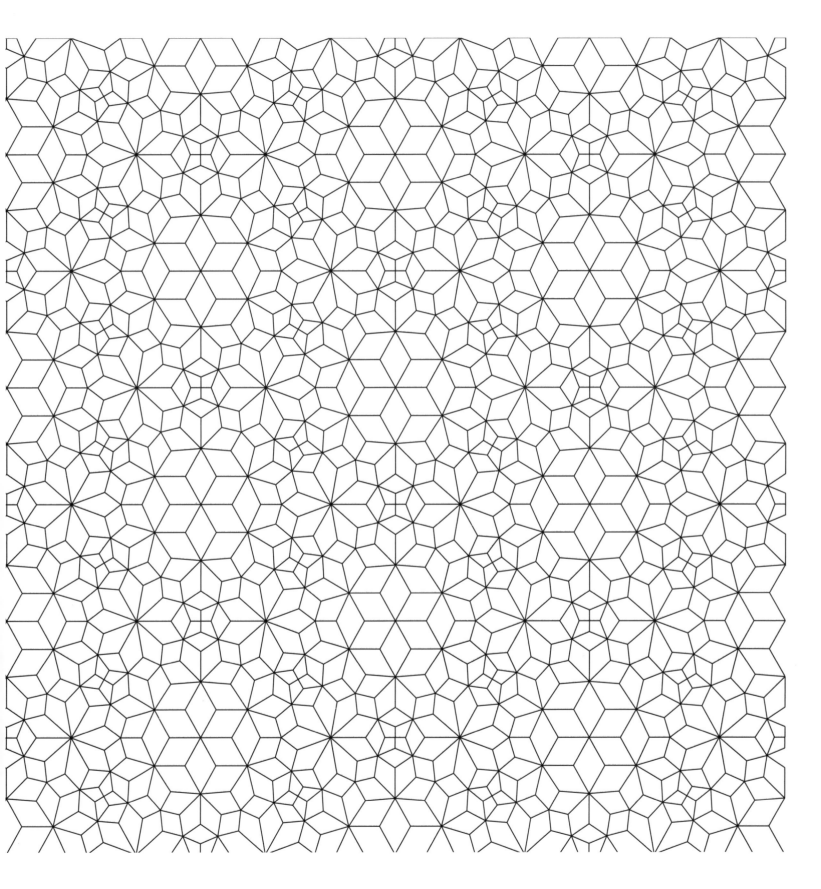

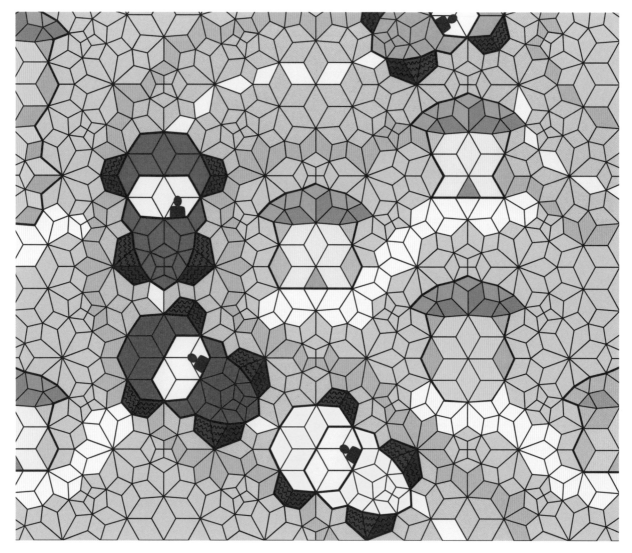

DESIGN # 8

Create a complete scene by finding cars, houses, and pathways in new positions in the design on the right.

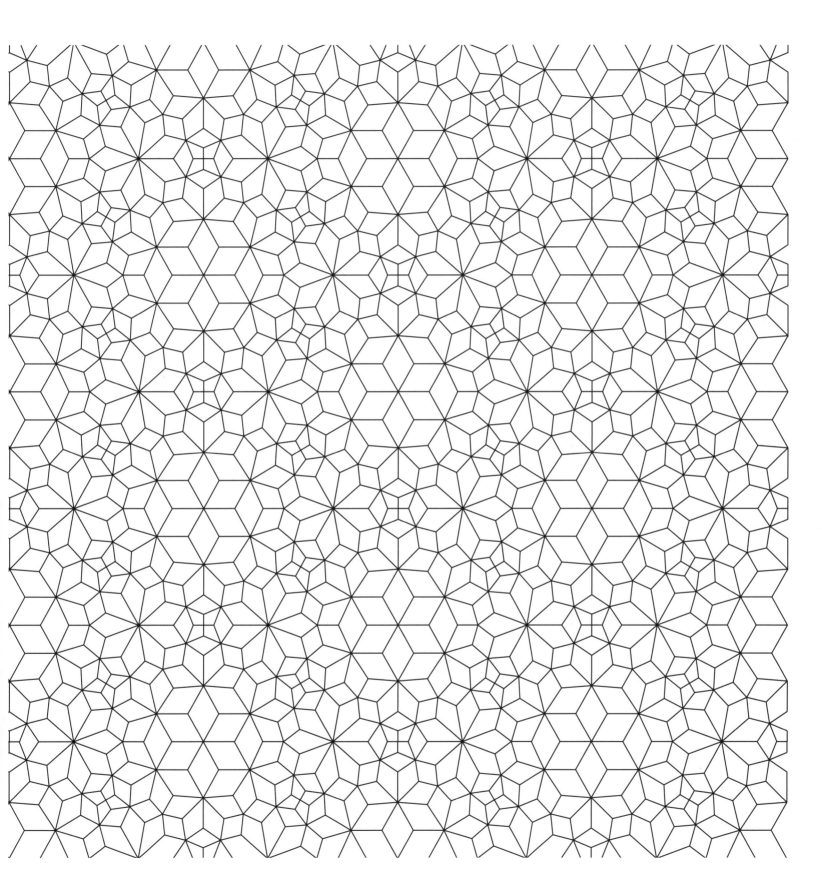

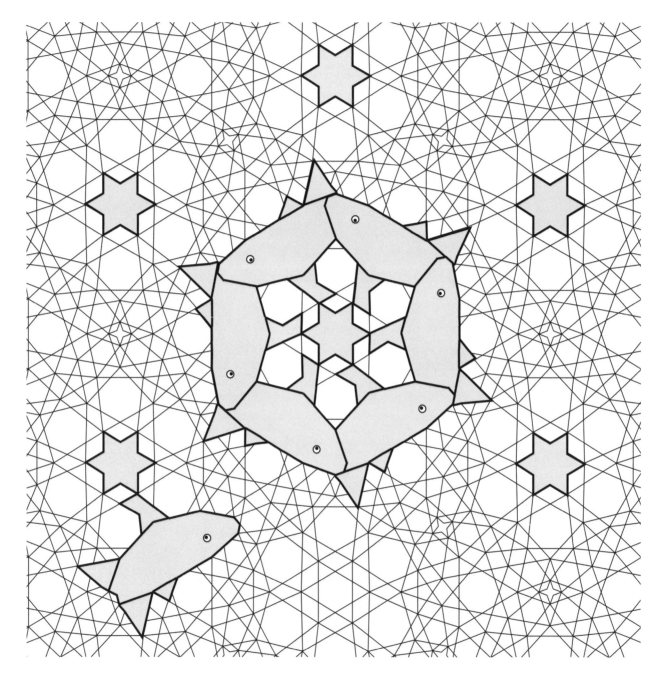

DESIGN # 9

Can you find rotating sharks in the design on the right?

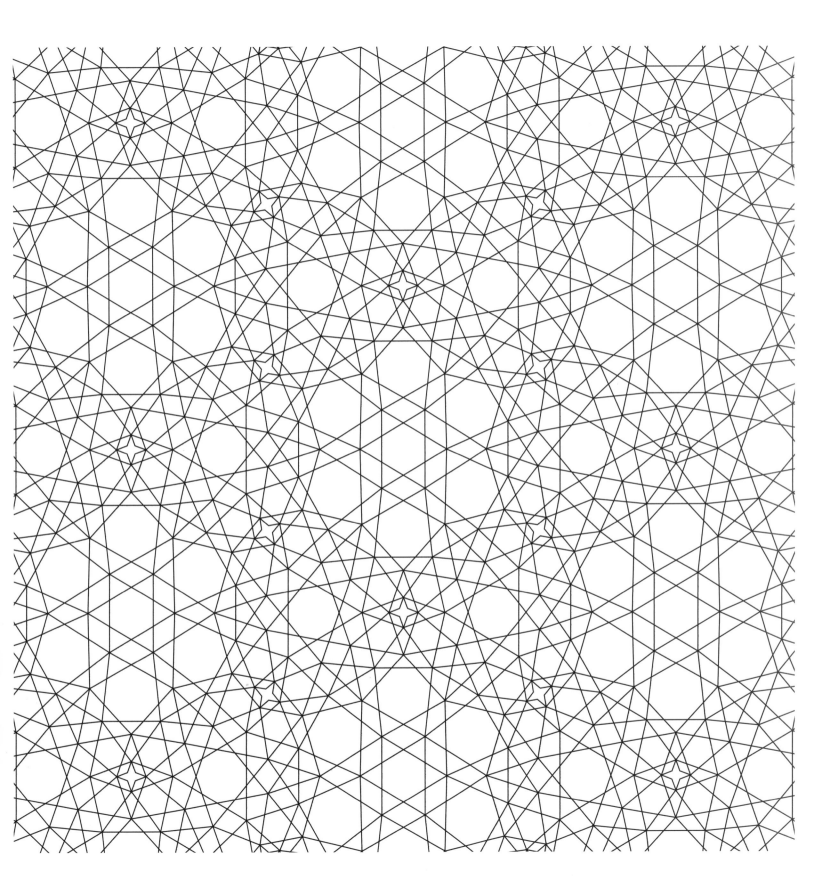

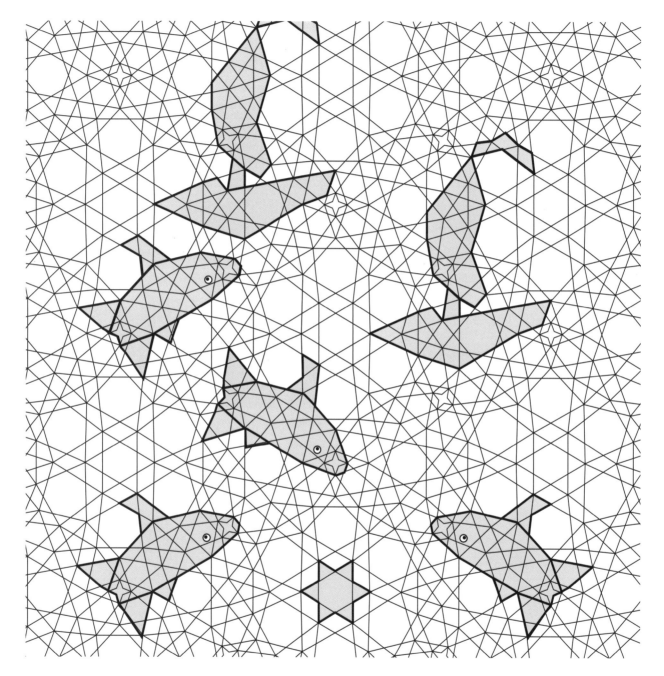

DESIGN # 9

Now that you found sharks, can you also find yachts?

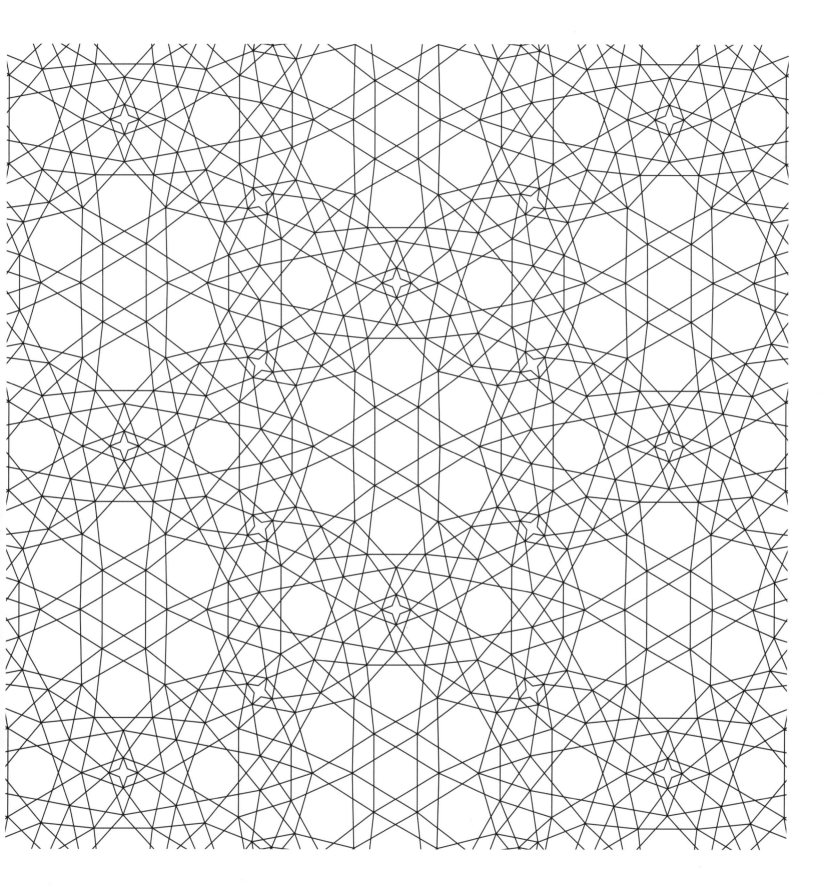

DESIGN # 9

Study the design to find your own shapes and images.

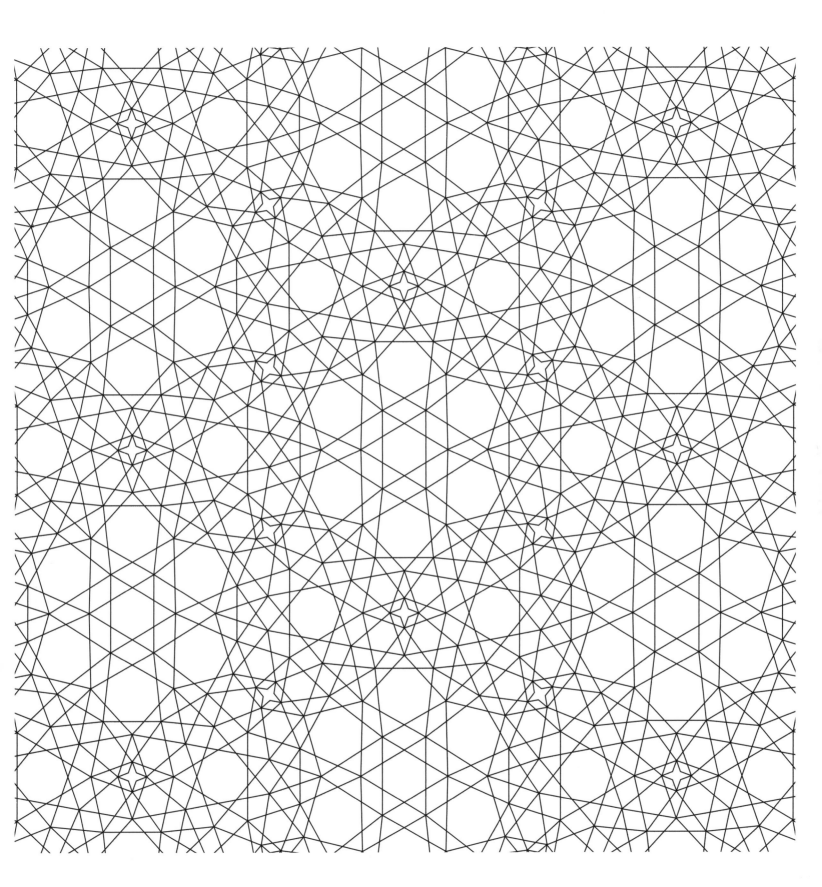

DESIGN # 9

Create a complete scene with all of the images that you find.

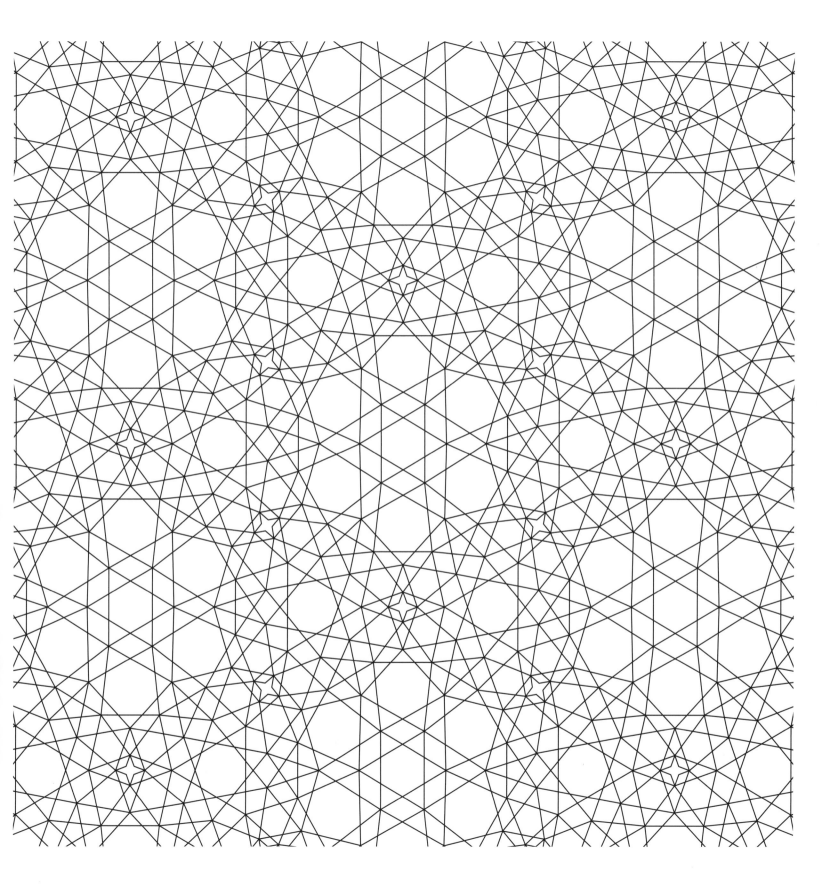

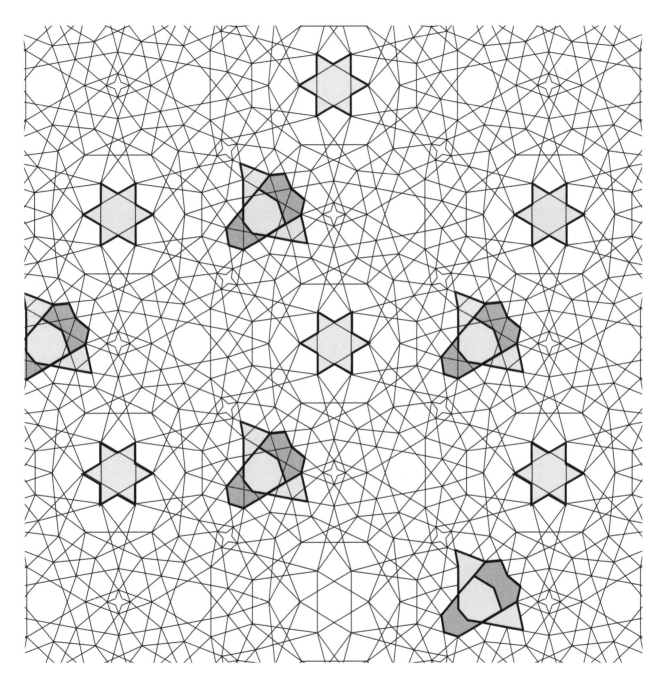

DESIGN # 10

When you find the six-sided stars, you can find the space shuttles flying next to them.

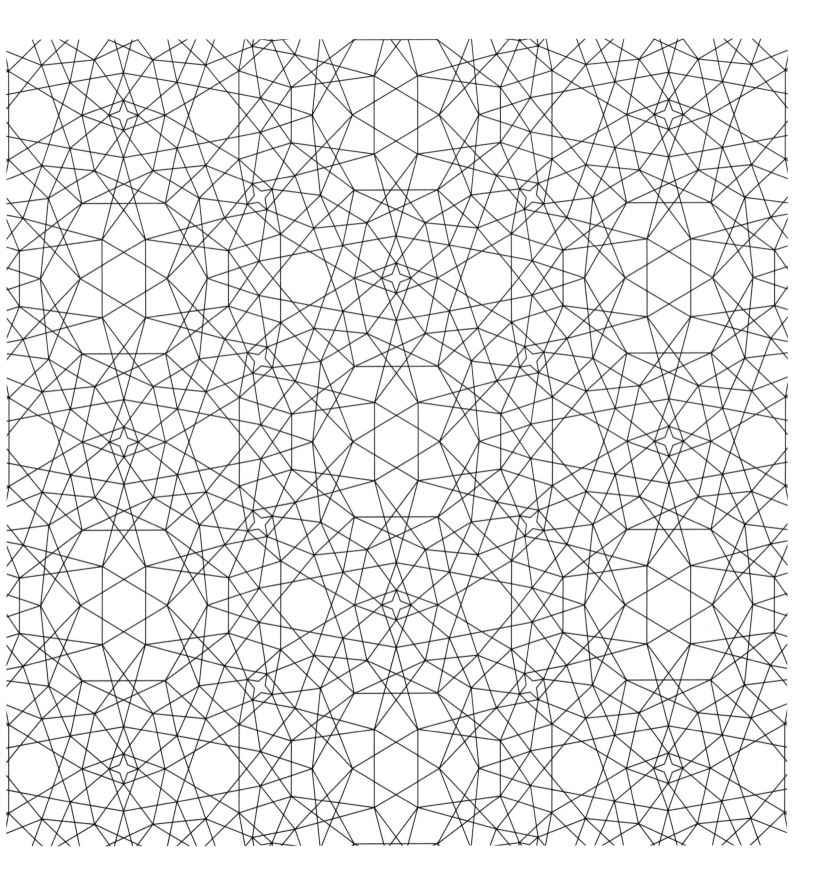

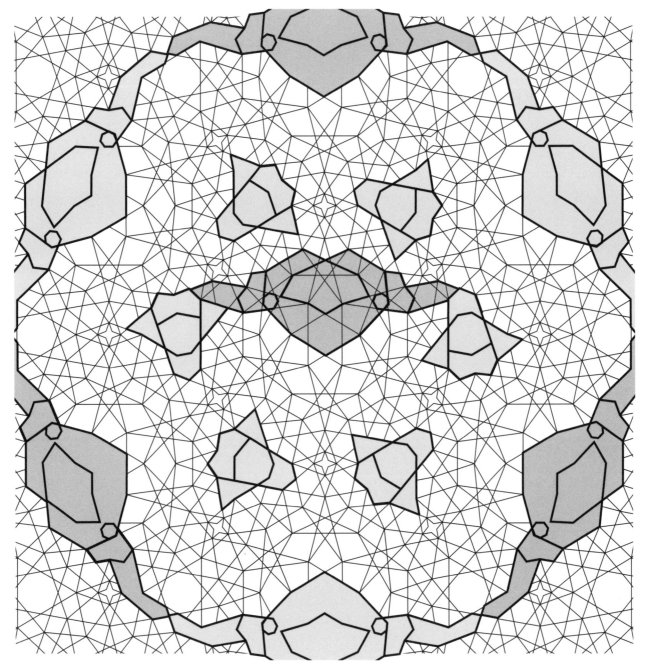

DESIGN # 10

Notice how the spaceships and space shuttles repeat and reflect.

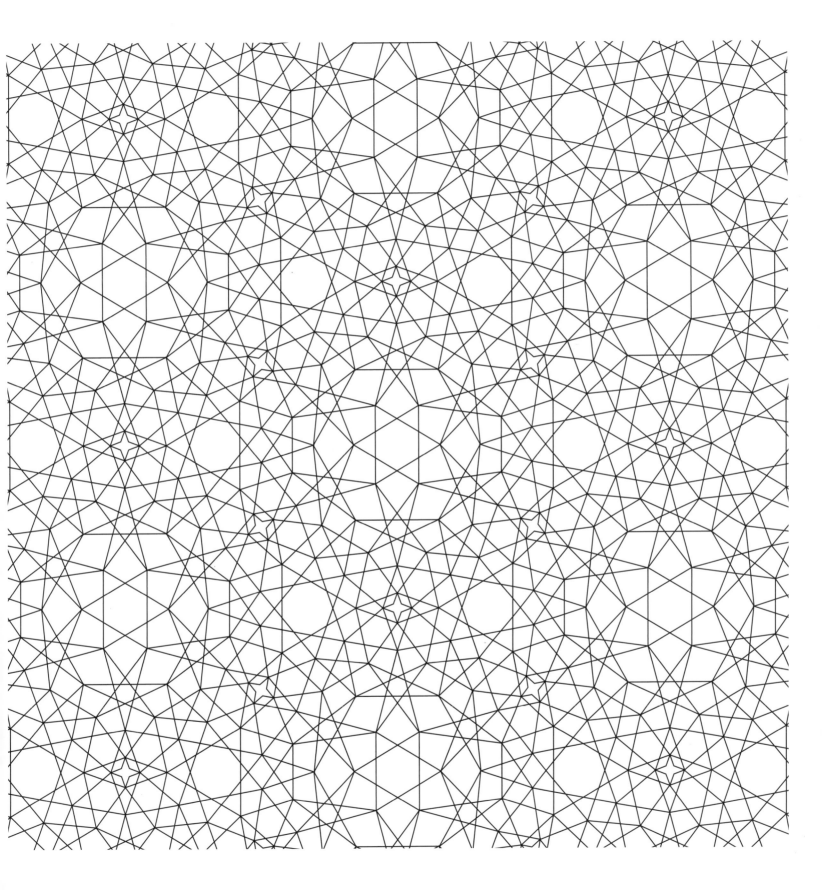

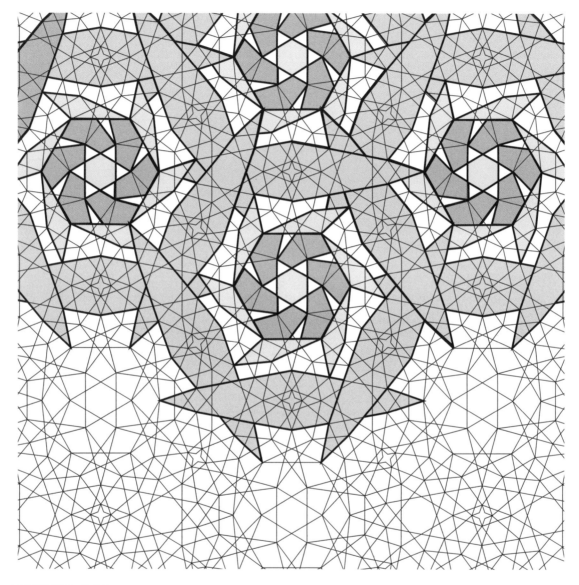

DESIGN # 10

What other images can you find in the patterns?

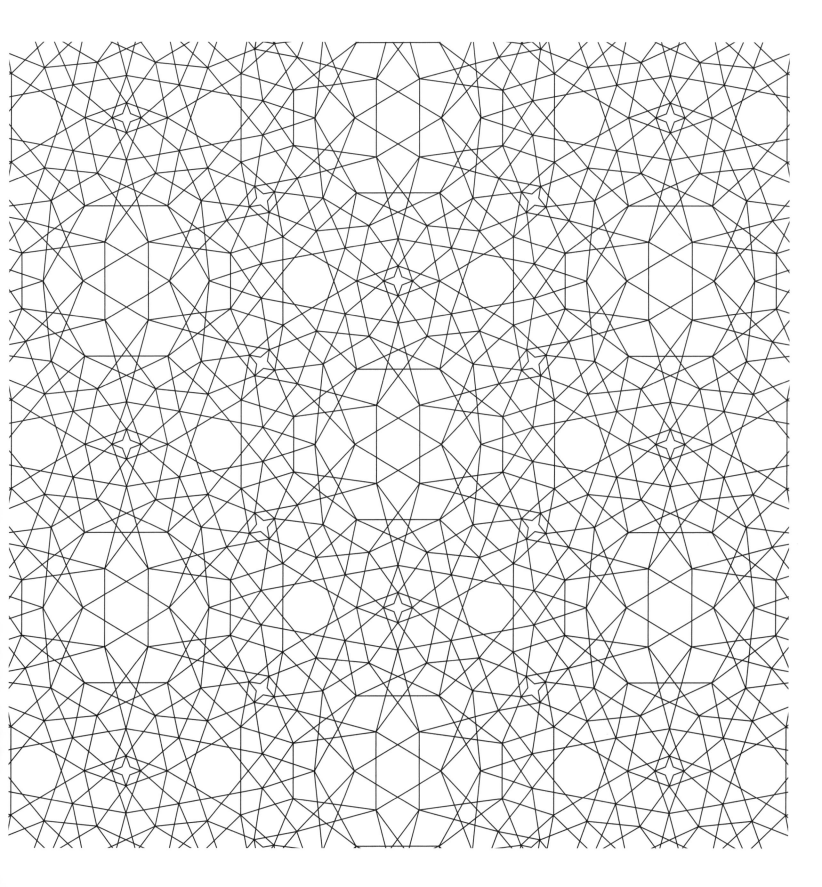

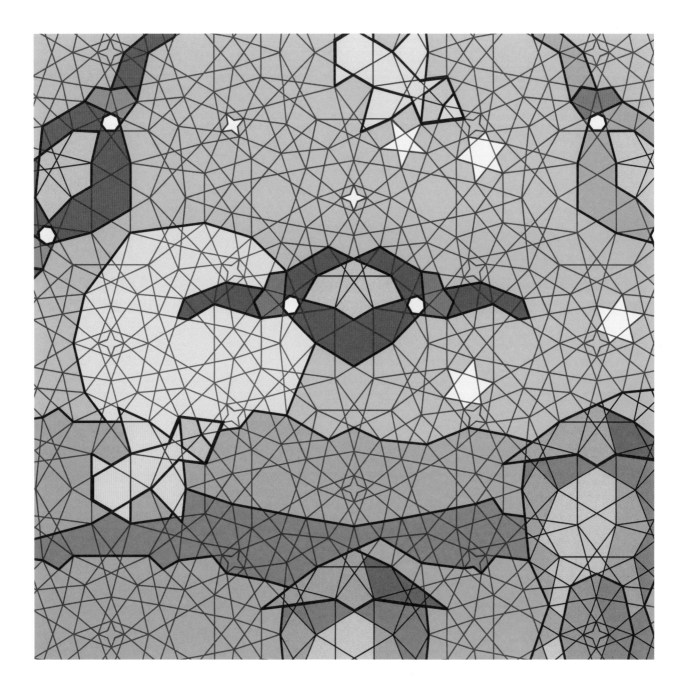

DESIGN # 10

Can you find a moon and houses to add to the scene in the design on the right?

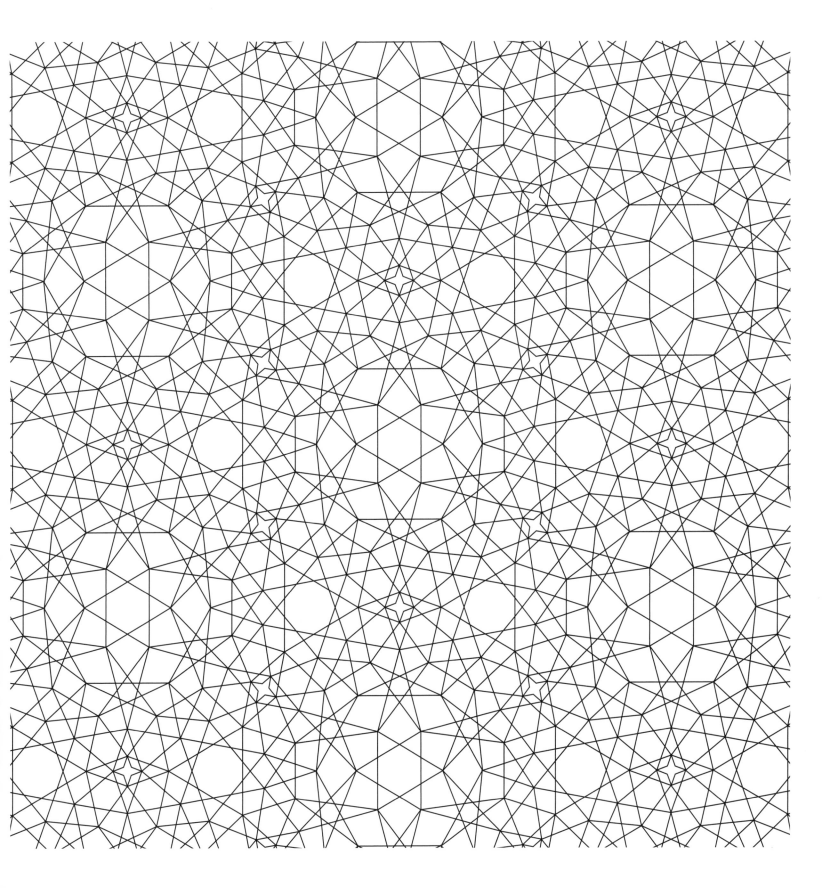

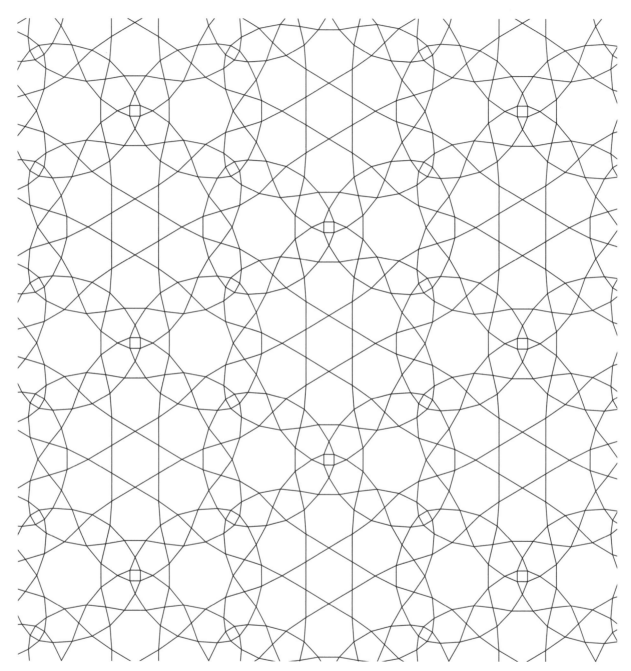

Now that you can find hidden images within a design, it's time to find some on your own. Use your imagination! What images do you see? How many images will you include? What completed scenes will you make? Find hidden images in the patterns on the left-side pages and create finished scenes on the right-side pages.

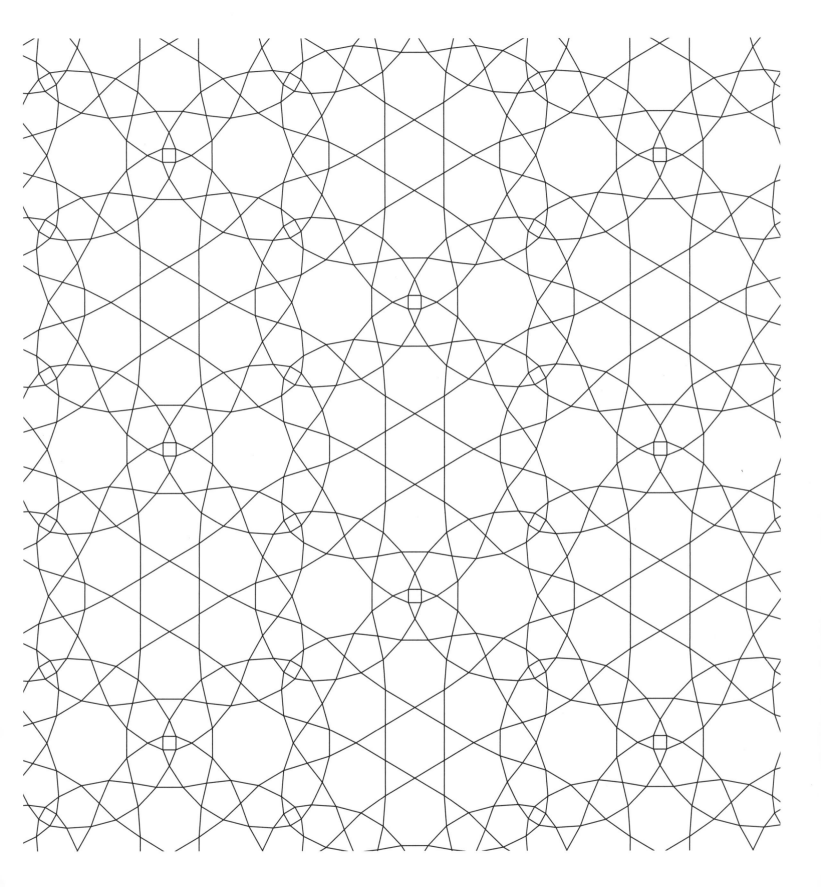

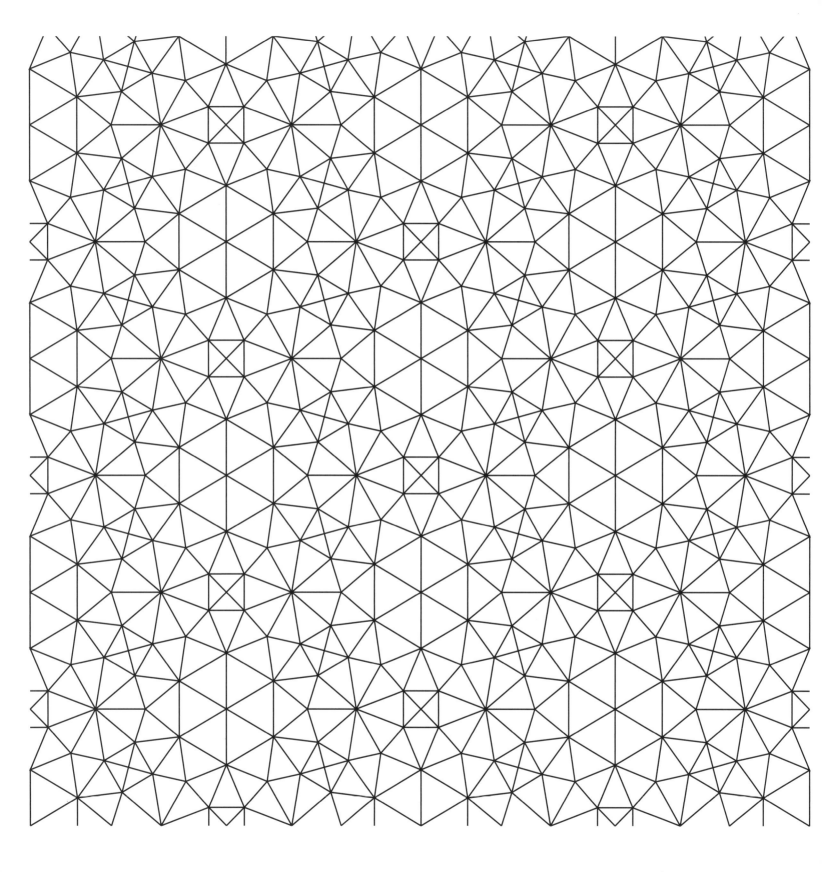

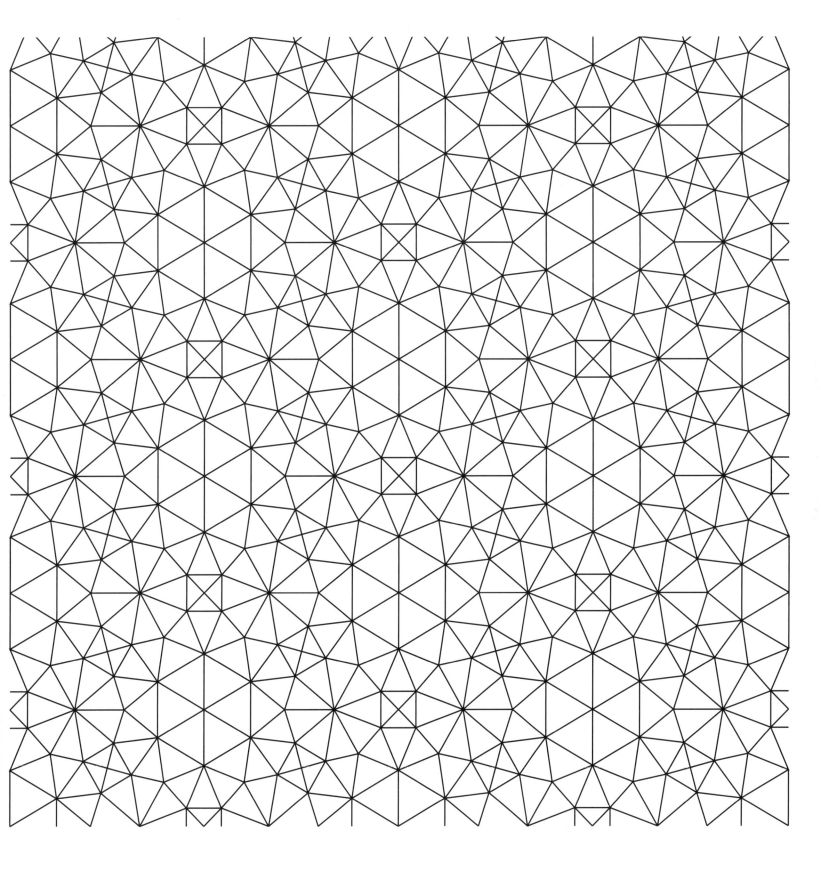

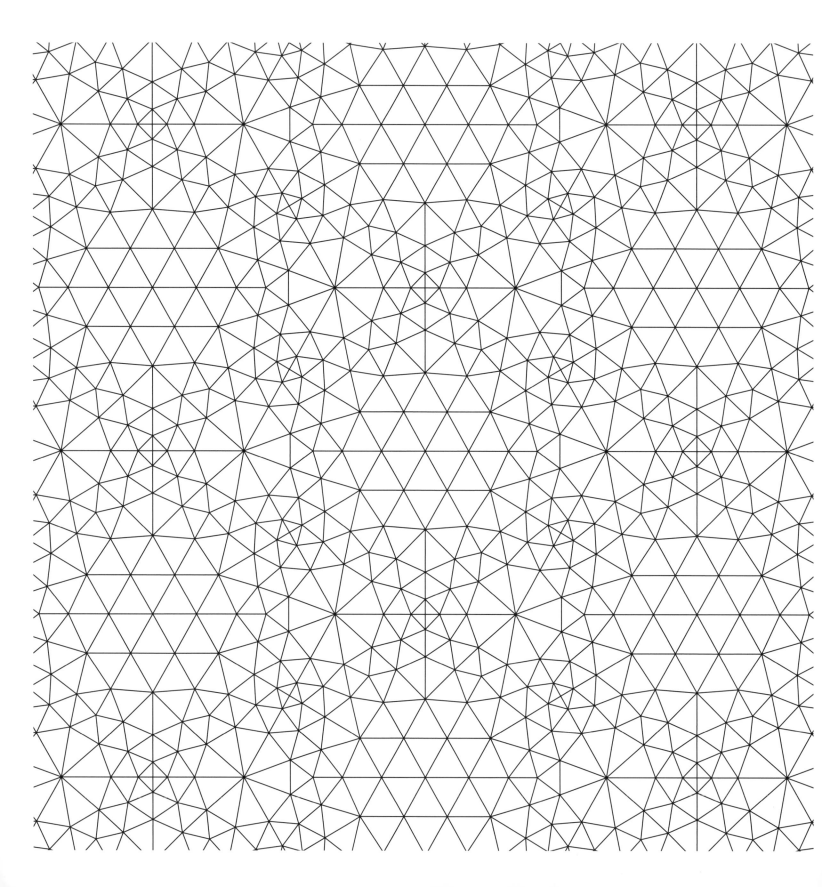

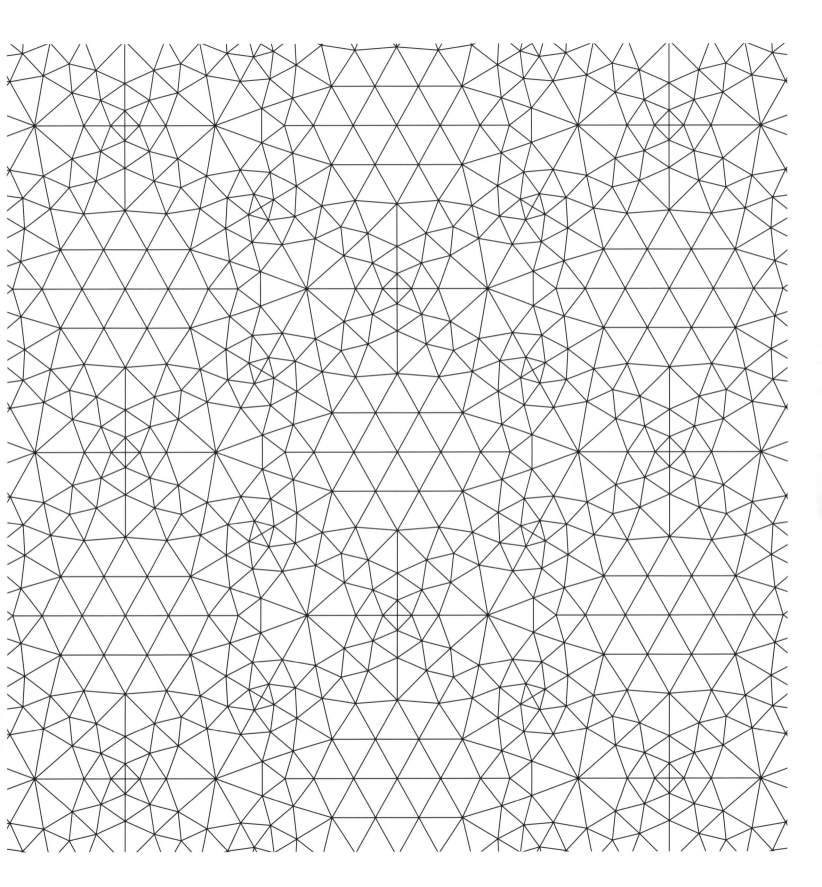

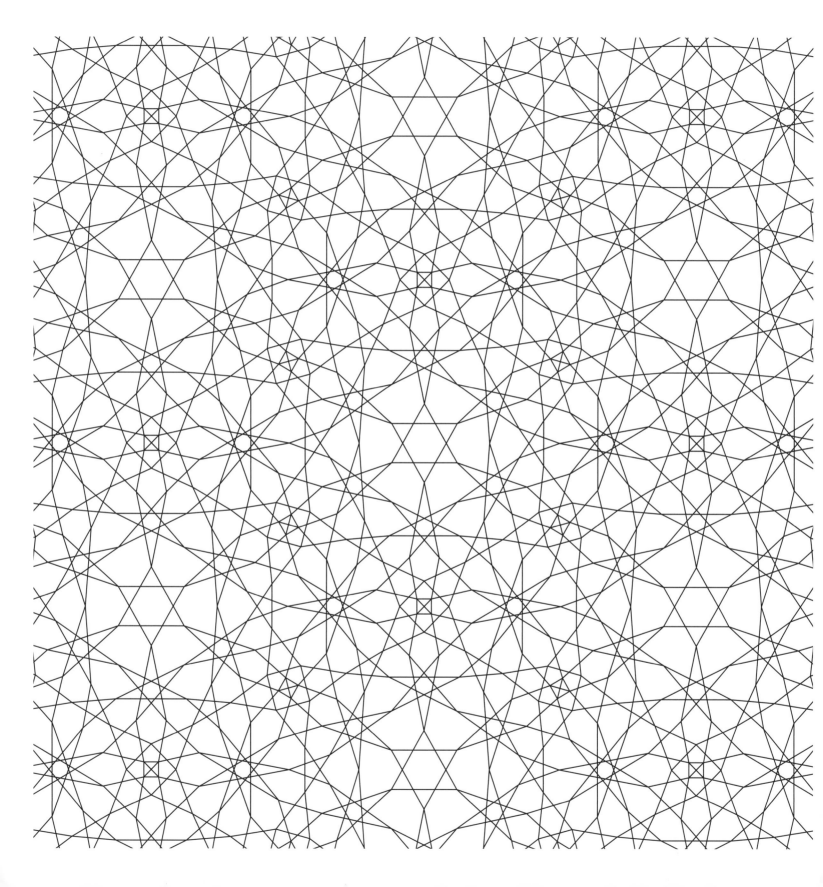

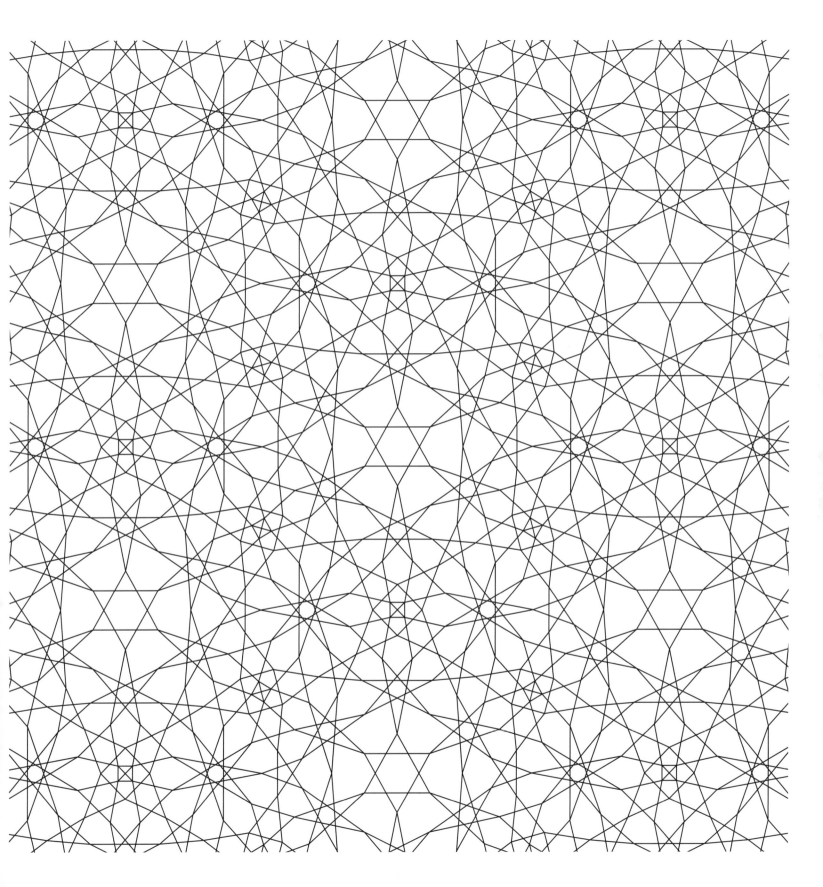

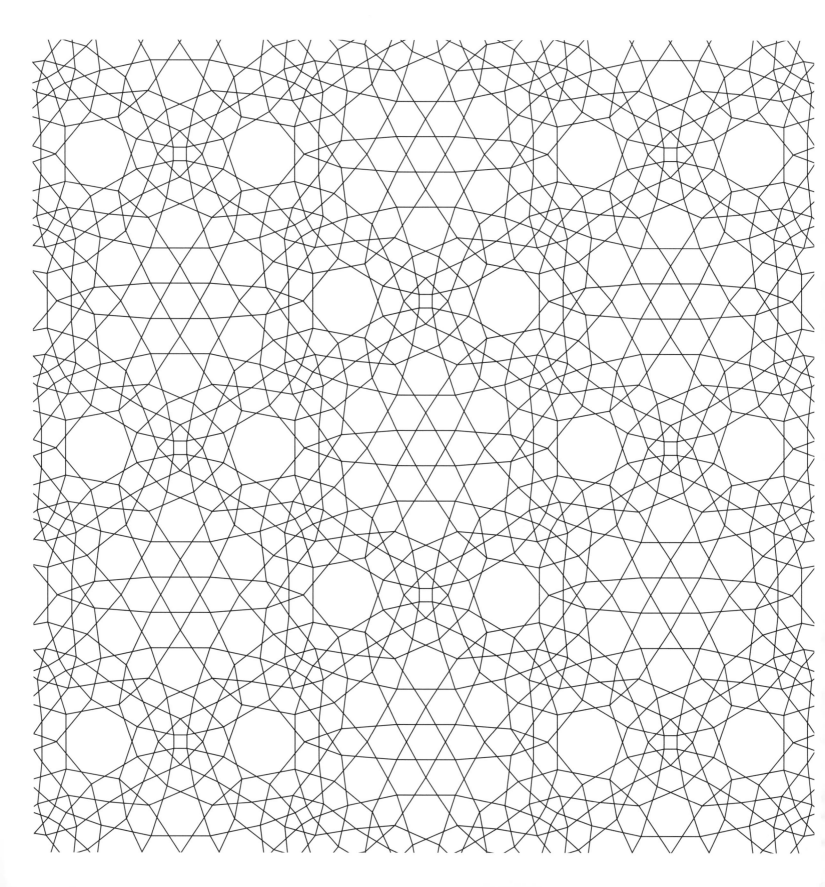

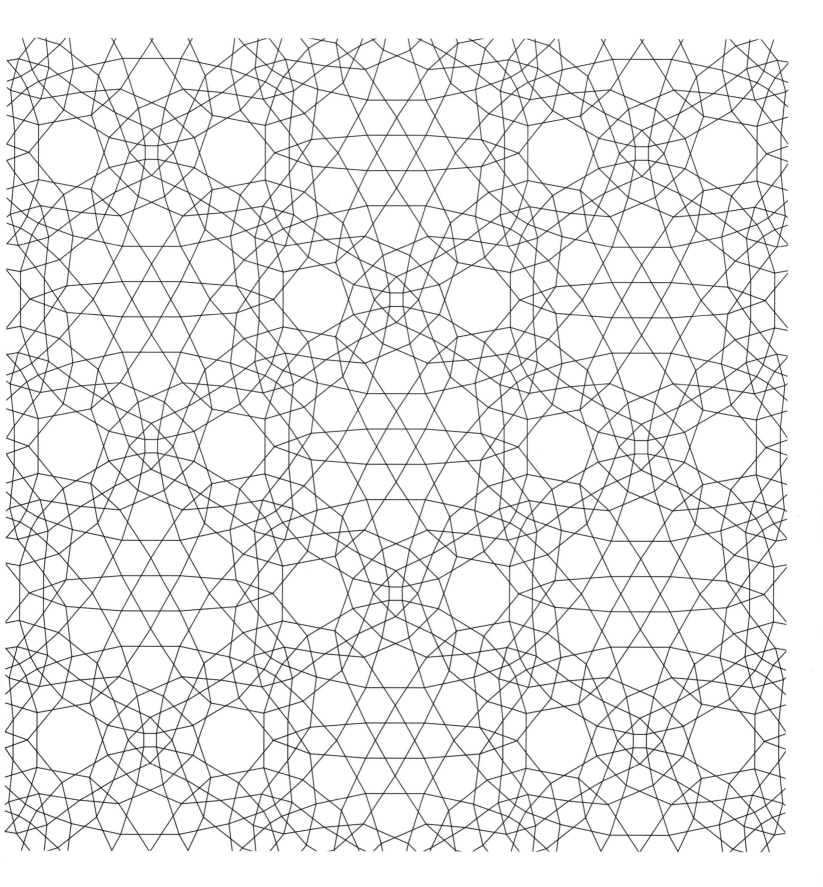

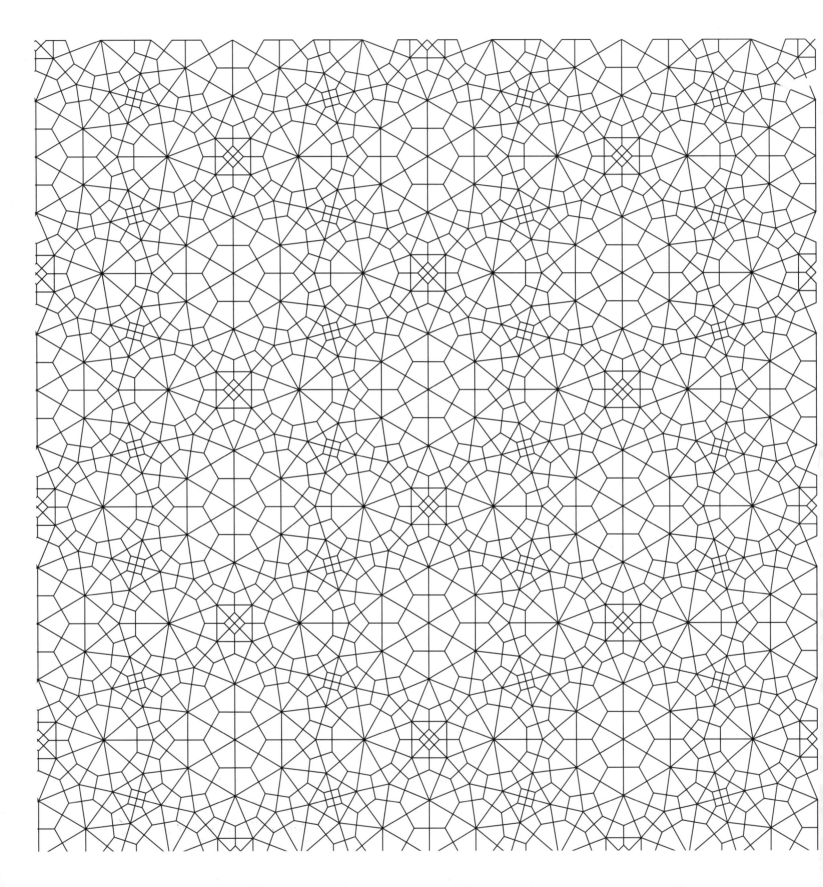